Berlitz®

Zákynthos & Kefalloniá

Text by Maria Lord
Picture Editor: Hilary Genin
Series Editor: Tony Halliday

Berlitz POCKET GUIDE
Zákynthos & Kefalloniá

First Edition 2004; Reprinted 2004

PHOTOGRAPHY
All photographs by Anna Mockford and Nick Bonnetti/Apa.
Cover: Indexstock.

CONTACTING THE EDITORS
Every effort has been made to provide accurate information in this publication, but changes are inevitable. The publisher cannot be responsible for any resulting loss, inconvenience or injury. We would appreciate it if readers would call our attention to any errors or outdated information by contacting Berlitz Publishing, PO Box 7910, London SE1 1WE, England. Fax: (44) 20 7403 0290;
e-mail: berlitz@apaguide.co.uk
www.berlitzpublishing.com

ACKNOWLEDGMENTS
The author would like to thank Nickey and María on Zákynthos, and Philip for help on Kefalloniá.

Flowers in bloom on the steep slopes overlooking charming Ásos (page 74), Kefalloniá ➤

The magnificent cave lake at Melissáni (page 65) is a highlight of Kefalloniá ◄

Zákynthos Museum (page 26) is home to many fine icons, frescoes and carvings ▼

TOP TEN ATTRACTIONS

e rugged
st coast
Zákynthos
ge 42) is an
spoilt region
raditional
villages

The breathtaking bay at
Andísamos (page 64), Kefalloniá,
was used as a location for the film
Captain Corelli's Mandolin

The winding west coast road of
Kefalloniá (page 73) has some of the
most spectacular views on the island

Watersports and beautiful beaches
make Vasilikós Peninsula (page 40),
Zákynthos, a popular location

genous firs cover the upper reaches
Kefalloniá's Mount Énos (page 62),
highest point in the Ionian islands

Swimming in
the Blue Caves
(page 47) of
Zákynthos is an
unforgettable
experience

The lovely Skaliá
Cultural Centre (page 35),
Zákynthos, holds story-
telling festivals in its
three outdoor theatres

CONTENTS

Fact Sheets

INTRODUCTION

The close neighbours of Zákynthos and Kefalloniá do, at first glance, share a great deal: history, geographical proximity and cultural influences. However, to listen to islanders talking you would think they were as different as chalk and cheese. The Zakynthians, according to themselves, are friendly, warm and outgoing, while the Kefallonians are aloof, reserved and suspicious; the Kefallonians, for their part, claim to be proud, independent and hospitable. For all these are stereotypes, imbued with a degree of local rivalry, there is a certain truth to all of the claims.

Even at the level of the landscape, Kefalloniá is more forbidding and mountainous than green, lush Zákynthos. As for the claim that the Zakynthians are more approachable than their neighbours, it is true that the large wave of emigration, and subsequent return of richer emigrés, has left a much more socially and geographically fractured society on Kefalloniá than on Zákynthos.

Both islands, however, are beautiful, and it is likely a visitor will find as much to admire in the wild, rugged west coast of Kefalloniá, as the cosy lowlands of the Central Plain on Zákynthos. Also strong on both islands is a long, vibrant cultural history, seen in their churches, painting and music.

The oft-quoted Venetian saying 'Zante, Fior di Levante' (Zante, Flower of the East; *see page 32*) refers to the east wind that carried the perfume of the island's many wild flowers – especially the now-endangered sea daffodils – miles out to sea. The Venetian sailors could therefore smell the island before it came into sight.

Mt Énos on Kefalloniá, viewed from Alikaná, Zákynthos

Geology and Environment

Another shared attribute of the islands is their important and unique natural environment. The sea around the islands is beautifully clean, crystal clear and home to two of the most endangered species to be found in Greek waters: the Mediterranean monk seal and the Mediterranean breeding population of the loggerhead turtle *(see pages 37–40)*.

Both islands are predominantly made of heavily folded Cretaceous limestones. Geologically they form a unit, separated from Corfu to the north by the Kefalloniá fault zone. On Zákynthos in particular the island's topography is easily related to the underlying geology. The western mountains are made of relatively hard Cretaceous limestones, while the gentler east is largely made up of Eocene deposits. The Vasilikós Peninsula is a combination of hard Triassic rocks and Plio-Pleistocene marls. Mountainous Kefalloniá largely comprises hard limestones, within which are numerous caves. The heavily folded rocks point to a turbulent geological

---

Mythical Origins

According to Greek mythology, Taphios, the son of Poseidon and Hippothoë, established the city of Taphos on the Peloponnese. Under his son Pterelaus this expanded to include the nearby Ionian islands, and so the inhabitants of Kefalloniá became known as Taphioi. The present-day name is said to come from Cephalus – a son of the king of Ileia – and the names of the four ancient cities *(see page 13)* from his four sons: Kranius, Paleus, Pronessos and Samos.

As for Zákynthos, Homer reported that Zakynthos was the son of King Dardanos on the Peloponnese. He settled on the island – thus giving it its name – and created the fortification of Psophidia, named after the town in Arcadia from which he came. It is possible that this was on the site of the present-day Bóhali *(see page 31)*.

Vineyards and fir trees near Póros, Kefalloniá

history, and the islands' location along the Hellenic Subduction Zone gives rise to numerous earthquakes.

As well as being home to several species of mammal (including martens, *Martes foina*, and, on Kefalloniá, feral ponies) the islands have a number of interesting reptiles. One of the most spectacular is the large, but harmless, Aesculapian snake *(Elaphe longissima)*, which can grow up to 2m (6½ft) in length. Birds include house martins *(Delichon urbica)* and the beautiful golden oriole *(Oriolus oriolus)*. Of the birds of prey look out for the tiny Scop's owl *(Otus scops)* and the much larger buzzard *(Buteo buteo)*.

The islands' flora is stunning, especially during spring. Kefalloniá is home to many rare wild flowers, including *Viola cephalonica* and *Campanula garganica-cephalonica*, as well as its own fir, *Abies cephalonica*. Zákynthos is an equally important habitat for flora, and still has populations of the fragrant sea daffodil *(Pancratium maritimum)*.

Tourism

On Zákynthos, the first package tourists arrived in 1982, brought by the British company Sunmed. Although there have been undoubted benefits for the islanders – largely an increase in personal wealth – there is also a downside. Indiscriminate development has spread along the south and east coast beaches of Zákynthos, bringing in its wake a huge annual influx of mostly British package tourists. Although they inject a considerable amount of cash into the local economy, much of the big money remains in the hands of the major tour operators and hotel owners. The tourists also bring social behaviour that is not necessarily welcomed by locals, including bouts of heavy drinking, and even the occasional fight.

As well as this social disturbance, there is a huge environmental impact from such a large number of visitors. Prior to the tourist boom the island was extremely poor, with its

The stunning, if dangerous, beach and sea at Mýrtos, Kefalloniá

infrastructure either destroyed or severely underdeveloped. Eager to exploit a steady source of income, locals threw up shoddy hotels and resorts with little regard for their environmental impact, never mind the water and sanitation needs of the annual 700,000 visitors. By the mid-1990s it was realised that action needed to be taken to protect certain headline species and to preserve still untouched sensitive areas. After a long, and occasionally bitter, campaign by local activists, the Marine National Park of Zákynthos was established in 1999 *(see pages 37–40)*.

Fiskárdo's attractive waterfront, Kefalloniá

The history of tourism on Kefalloniá is less invasive. It has, so far, largely escaped the ravages of mass package tourism that have afflicted parts of Zákynthos. The relatively low-key tourist developments that do exist are mainly concentrated in Lássi on the west coast, and Skála in the south. The real boost to Kefalloniá's tourism industry came in the mid-1990s with the phenomenal success of the book *Captain Corelli's Mandolin* by Louis de Bernières *(see page 67)*. The descriptions of (pre-war) idyllic island life inspired a large number of visitors to come and see for themselves. Generally fairly affluent, these visitors (mainly from Italy and the UK) have encouraged high-end, and therefore more expensive, development. These tend to be visually kinder to the landscape, though there is a danger of some places, Fiskárdo in particular, becoming overly twee.

Island Life

Though both islands suffer an annual invasion, away from the tourist hordes, and outside the peak months of July and August, life carries on much as it does elsewhere in Greece. Many people still have land that is farmed for olives and grapes, and the harvest for both takes place during the autumn and winter.

Celebrating Ionian Union Day in Argostóli, Kefalloniá

A number of the local *tavérnes* stay open throughout the winter, and this is the time when islanders tend to go out and enjoy themselves after the hard work of the tourist season. This division of the year does lead to high seasonal unemployment, and some people move to the mainland during the winter. Aside from fishing and agriculture there is little else in terms of industry on either Zákynthos or Kefalloniá – the odd quarry or small-scale food processing – and there has been talk of trying to expand the tourist season, such as offering spring treks to see the islands' flora, in an effort to spread income more evenly across the year.

One traditional aspect of life that still continues is the singing of *kandádes*. These are songs performed by a group of male singers with guitar accompaniment. The music itself is a combination of local traditional songs, Italian popular songs and 19th-century operatic arias (a legacy of Venetian rule). It is not at all unusual to hear Neapolitan favourites such as *O sole mio* in among the Greek offerings. *Arékia*, also popular, is a similar but more thoughtful solo song genre.

A BRIEF HISTORY

Evidence of early human settlement on the southern Ionian islands is scarce. There has been little excavation of specifically palaeolithic and neolithic sites, though a number of artefacts, such as flint hand tools (for example scrapers) have been found, some of which are on display in Argostóli's archaeological museum. The earliest human presence is thought to date from the mid-Palaeolithic era (c.50,000 years ago), when, due to ice-age reduction in sea levels, the Ionians were joined to present-day Greece and Italy. It is thought that hunting groups arrived in the region, probably searching for food, from the Píndos (northern Greece) and the Peloponnese. These groups then settled on what are now the islands of Zákynthos and Kefaloniá.

The Bronze Age

Archaeologists now know that there was a thriving Mycenean society on Kefaloniá. As yet, aside from the Bronze-Age tombs close to Kabí on the west coast, there is little corresponding evidence from Zákynthos. It is assumed, backed up by artefacts found during excavations, that the four city states of ancient Kefaloniá *(see box, right)* have their origins in the Late-Helladic period of c.1500–1050BC. One of the major centres on Kefaloniá appears to have been near Tzanáta in the southeast, about 8km (5 miles) from the site of Pronnoi, of interest due to its possible links

> **Ancient Kefaloniá was a Tetrapolis, ie it comprised four independent city-states. These were: Pali on present-day Pallikí, Krani near Drápano, Sami near the port of the same name, and Pronnoi in the south of the island.**

The Mycenean tholos tomb near Tzanáta, Kefalloniá

to Odysseus *(see pages 15 and 68)*. Other important sites on Kefalloniá include: the chamber tombs at Mazarakáta, first excavated by C.P. de Bosset in 1813; the Late-Helladic chamber tombs at Metaxáta; and the Late-Helladic chamber tomb at Lakíthra, which yielded the richest finds of any of the island's Bronze-Age tombs.

The Archaic, Classical and Hellenic Periods

The origins of the city-states of Kefalloniá and the early rulers of Zákynthos are the subjects of Greek mythology *(see page 8)*. However, there are more recent historical references; Zákynthos and the four city-states of Kefalloniá were mentioned by both Herodotus and Thucydides. Zákynthos seems to have been an independent region, ruled by leaders who originally came from the Peloponnese, possibly nearby Achaia. This independence lasted until just before the outbreak of the Peloponnesian War (431BC), when the island was conquered by the Athenian general Tolmides; it was hence on the side of Athens during most of the conflict.

The pattern on Kefalloniá was more complex. The city-states were generally politically independent of each other and formed their own alliances; Pali alone fought in the Persian Wars, at the battle of Plataea (479BC). However, up until the Peloponnesian War they were all to a greater or lesser extent – but particularly Pali – allied to Corinth. Krani also had links to the Athenians and, on the outbreak of the Peloponnesian War, the whole island was brought under the sphere of Athens.

At some point during the archaic and Classical periods (from c.750BC) the Kefallonian city-states became democratic. Professor G. Moschopoulos notes that the Kefallonian *demos* (citizens eligible to vote – this excluded women and slaves) took part in political decision-making, and that the *vouli* (the city parliament) was the 'dominant institution' in the city of Pali. He also points out that none of the coins from the city-states showed an image of a ruler (except for that of the mythical founder Cephalus; *see page 8*).

Towards the end of the Peloponnesian War Zákynthos fell under the sphere of Sparta, while the Kefallonian cities wavered in their allegiance between Sparta and Athens, and in

Odysseus

The Homeric epic *The Odyssey* follows the adventures of its eponymous hero from Troy, on the coast of Anatolia, back home to mythical Ithaca. For a long time it was assumed that Ithaca was present-day Itháki, and numerous local features were named after events in the epic. However, there is no archaeological evidence to back these claims, and the latest thinking points to southern Kefalloniá as the most likely spot for the kingdom. Zákynthos is completely out of the running, although it is mentioned by name in both *The Odyssey* and *The Iliad*.

226BC became a member of the Aetolic marine confederation. Later, both islands came to the attention of the Macedonians. Philip V occupied Zákynthos – and temporarily lost the island to the Romans during the 2nd Punic War (218–202BC) – but failed to conquer Kefalloniá. The end of Hellenistic influence came when the Romans, under Marcus Fulvius Nobili, conquered Zákynthos in 191BC and Kefalloniá in 189BC.

The Byzantines and Franks

From the point of the Roman invasion to the advent of Byzantine rule in 337AD little of note is recorded in the history of either island. However, the archaeological record shows a certain degree of wealth and artisitic activity, as at the villa at Skála on Kefalloniá *(see page 62)*. Under the Byzantines the islands, Kefalloniá in particular, became active in defending the empire against attack from Arab pirates, and, in 850, Kefalloniá became the head of a *thema*, or administrative district. Zákynthos fared less well during this period, and the sacking of the island by the Vandals in 474 was the first of a number of attacks by outside forces.

As the power of the Byzantines waned, attacks on both islands became more common. In 1085 Robert Guiscard, a Norman leader, attacked Fiskárdo on Kefalloniá, and by 1185 the island was under the rule of the Franks (a disparate group of largely Norman and Italian fiefdoms). In 1204, after the sacking of Constantinople during the infamous Fourth Crusade, Zákynthos followed suit and remained under Frankish rule until 1479. The Frankish rulers of Kefalloniá were a diverse group, at first headed by the Venetian Orsini family, to whom it passed after the Fourth Crusade. In 1357 it was passed, by the King of Naples, to the Tocco family, the most remarkable member of which was Francesca, wife of Carlo I, who reigned after his death, setting up a court of women in Kástro Agíou Georgíou *(see page 58)*.

The Ottomans and Venetians

With the growing power of the Ottoman Turks to the east, it was inevitable that the islands would soon receive their attention, and, in 1479, Zákynthos and Kefalloniá were attacked by Ahmad Pasha. The Ottomans overran the islands, taking many prisoners back to Istanbul. Although the Venetians, then the other major force in the eastern Mediterranean, regained Kefalloniá in 1481, it was ceded back to Sultan Beyazit II in a treaty in 1485.

The Venetians were not deterred from ideas of Mediterranean domination, however, and in 1489 invaded and took over control of Zákynthos. Eleven years later, in 1500, they attacked Kefalloniá with the help of a Spanish army, and, after a two-month siege, took control of Kástro Agíou Georgíou on Christmas Day. Thus, apart from a brief period, the islands are among the few areas of Greece not to have

The Venetian fort at Ásos, Kefalloniá

> 'The reason they build
> their houses so lowe
> [on Zákynthos] is,
> because of the manifold
> Earthquakes which
> doe as much share
> this Iland as any other
> place in the World.'
> Thomas Coryat, 1612

come under, and been influenced by, Ottoman rule.

The two islands remained under the Venetians until 1797. This was a period of relative calm, although the Venetians ensured that both Zákynthos and Kefalloniá were heavily defended; the impressive castles at Bóhali on Zákynthos, and Ásos and Agíou Geórgiou (the long-time Venetian capital) on Kefalloniá are mainly a legacy of Venetian rule. Not only were the islands prized as important staging posts for the Venetian navy, they were also useful for their agricultural production, and most of the many olive trees now seen on the islands were planted during this time.

One of the most visible legacies of the Venetian occupation is the large number of splendid churches, many with ornate, gilded baroque interiors, found on the islands. Much of the churches' interior decoration, and many of their icons, is the work of Cretan sculptors and painters, who fled to Zákynthos and Kefalloniá after Crete fell to the Ottomans in 1669. Once on the two Ionian islands, they came under the influence of the Italian Renaissance and the resulting artistic synthesis is known as Ionian School painting.

The local rulers came from Venetian aristocratic families, who acquired large estates and settled on the islands. Their names were inscribed in what was called the *Libro d'Oro* (Golden Book). With the greater exposure to the Western world, a number of schools, mostly for religious instruction, were established, bringing the teachings of the enlightenment to the islands. For all this, they were still under autocratic rule, and people were not immune from the rumblings of nationalist discontent that grew steadily in the 18th century.

The Septinsular Republic and the British

This discontent became evident when, in 1797, the islands were occupied by the revolutionary French. The heartening revolutionary fervour with which the islanders greeted the invaders – the *Libro d'Oro* was burnt in Argostóli's main square – initially went into radical proposals such as the abolition of religion. However, the rival powers, specifically the Orthodox Russians, were not at all happy about Napoleon's widening sphere of influence and agitation against the French began to ferment. In 1798 a joint Russian and Turkish fleet sailed for the islands and, with local support, they fell easily to the invaders.

The subsequent Treaty of Constantinople, signed in 1800, ushered in the creation of an autonomous republic under Turkish suzerainty. This, the Eptánisos Politía (or Septinsular Republic), became the first, nominally, independent modern Greek state. Not all went smoothly, however, particularly

Iconostasis from the church of Pandokrátora, Zákynthos Museum

on Kefalloniá, where Argostóli and Lixoúri were engaged in bitter, sometimes violent, rivalry for political dominance.

The fledgling state came to an end in 1807, when the islands passed back to the French under the Treaty of Tilsit, and in turn Zákynthos and Kefalloniá were occupied by the British in 1809. The British occupation, which lasted until 1863, was not an entirely happy time for the islanders. Although the British did carrry out a number of public works (such as building the Ágios Georgíos lighthouse and Drápano bridge near Argostóli), the local population became increasingly unhappy about foreign occupation and rule, especially after the creation of the neighbouring modern Greek state in 1828–32. Although the largely complicit urban middle class had a comfortable standard of living, the peasant farmers were oppressed and poor and, on Kefalloniá in 1848–9, they staged two armed revolts against British rule.

Zákynthos Town in the 19th century, depicted by Joseph Cartwright

Independence

The two islands had long been a place of refuge for independence fighters from the mainland (the military leader Kolokotronis had landed on Zákynthos in 1805), and in 1863 the islanders' nationalist ambitions were finally realised when the London Protocol declared the Ionian islands part of Greece.

Dionysios Solomos *(see page 29)*

The enlightenment ideals that had spurred the islanders to agitate for independence manifested themselves post-1863 in radical politics. Kefalloniá in particular was a hotbed of dissent and was the home of Marinos Antypas, the 'first Greek socialist', who was murdered in Thessaly in 1907. A more disturbing side of this penchant for radicalism came through in the facist dictator Ioannnis Metaxas, a native of Kefalloniá, who ruled Greece from a military coup in 1936 until his death in 1941, two months before the German invasion of Greece.

World War II and the 1953 Earthquake

The next 15 years or so were a period of great hardship for the islands, resulting in a large number of families leaving for Australia, the US and South Africa. The first catastrophe was World War II. Although the Greeks initially repulsed and held Mussolini's forces in 1940–41, more powerful joint Axis forces overran the country during 1941. Zákynthos and Kefalloniá were initially under the Italians, but when Italy capitulated in 1943 the Germans invaded, imposed a more brutal regime and, on Kefalloniá, executed most of the Italian soldiers (as told in *Captain Corelli's Mandolin, see page 67*).

The islands had just begun to recover from the joint effects of World War II and the ensuing Greek Civil War when, in August 1953, they were struck by a huge earthquake. The epicentre was on the seabed between Zákynthos and Kefalloniá, so the impact was felt more in the southern, settled parts of Kefalloniá, and the northern part of Zákynthos, which was relatively unpopulated. The devastation on Kefalloniá was almost total and over 400 people were killed. Zákynthos town was also completely destroyed, not only by the quake itself, but by fire and explosions, due in part to cooking fires and the practice of keeping – illegally – a box of dynamite under the bed to help with illicit fishing.

The Arrival of Tourism

Many people from the richer island of Kefalloniá emigrated. Far fewer left Zákynthos, and this island in particular suffered a period of great poverty which only began to lift when, in 1982, the first package tourists arrived. This sparked a wave of indiscriminate tourist development, spreading like a rash along the sandy beaches of the south and east coasts. Kefalloniá was relatively ignored until

A mural of Captain Corelli in Sámi

the phenomenal success of *Captain Corelli's Mandolin* brought tourists to the island in the 1990s, at the same time as emigré Kefallonians began to return from abroad. The environmental dangers of tourism have become more than evident, though the tide may have started to turn, with the creation of the first marine national park on Zákynthos in 1999.

Historical Landmarks

c.50,000BC Evidence of palaeolithic settlement.

c.1500–1050BC Establishment of the four city states of Kefalloniá.

431BC Outbreak of Peloponnesian War.

191–189BC Conquest of the islands by the Romans.

AD337 The islands come under Byzantine rule.

1185–1479 Frankish occupation of the islands.

1479 Ottomans overrun the islands, taking many locals prisoner.

1489–1500 The Ottomans are driven from the islands (Zákynthos: 1489; Kefalloniá: 1500) by Venetians, never to return. This ensures that the islands are among the few areas of Greece to remain free of Ottoman control and influence.

1500–1797 Era of Venetian rule leads to the appearance of distinctive churches and olive plantations.

1797 The islands are occupied by the revolutionary French.

1798 Russians and Turks, unhappy at Napoleon's widening influence, mount a joint expedition and take the islands from French.

1800 Treaty of Constantinople. The Eptánisos Politía becomes the first autonomous modern Greek state, albeit under Turkish suzerainty.

1807 Treaty of Tilsit. The islands pass back to the French.

1809–63 British occupation of the islands.

1848–9 Two armed revolts against British rule by peasant farmers.

1863 The London Protocol declares the Ionian islands part of Greece.

1941–3 World War II. Greece is occupied initially by Italians, then Germans. Nazi executions of Italian soldiers on Kefalloniá later form inspiration for *Captain Corelli's Mandolin*.

1953 A huge earthquake hits Kefalloniá and Zákynthos, destroying almost all buildings and killing over 400 people.

1982 First package tours arrive on Zákynthos.

1999 National Marine Park of Zákynthos is established.

2000 The movie of *Captain Corelli's Mandolin*, starring Penélope Cruz and Nicholas Cage, is filmed on Kefalloniá.

2004 Greece hosts the Olympic Games.

ZÁKYNTHOS

Zákynthos, also known by its Italian name Zante, is the southernmost of the seven Ionian islands that lie off the western coast of mainland Greece. The island divides into three geographical areas: the Vasilikós Peninsula in the southeast, a central plain, and the wild and mountainous north and west. One of the greenest of all the Greek islands, it has good, fertile soil and receives a generous amount of rain in the winter and early spring.

Although Zákynthos is now thoroughly Greek, evidence of the island's Venetian heritage is inescapable, from its Italianate church towers, to the descendants of aristocratic Venetian families, still major landowners.

> While Zákynthos's beautiful sandy beaches, concentrated on its southern and eastern coasts, are predominantly popular with package holidaymakers, the rest of the island – especially the area along the west coast – remains rugged and, for the most part, undeveloped.

ZÁKYNTHOS TOWN

The once-elegant harbour town of Zákynthos had its public buildings and squares rebuilt approximately as they were before the 1953 earthquake, but in reinforced concrete. Ferries from Kyllíni pull in at the long jetty at the southern end of the harbour, where the port authority can also be found.

Running parallel to the harbour is the main shopping street of Alex. Románou where you will find most of the up-market boutiques and jewellers. Románou ends at Platía Agíou Márkou, which ajoins Platía Solomoú.

Zákynthos' Blue Caves near Cape Skinári

The Zákynthos Museum

Platía Solomoú is the focus of the northern end of the harbourfront, and the town's museums and municipal buildings are clustered around it. On the square is the Zákynthos Museum, also known as the **Museum of Post-Byzantine Art** (open Tues–Sun 8am–2.30pm; entrance fee). It contains many pieces from the old Pandokrátora Museum, as well as frescoes, icons and carvings rescued from churches devastated in the 1953 earthquake. There are also 17th- to 19th-century religious paintings of the Ionian School, founded by Cretan artists fleeing the Ottoman conquest who met local artists strongly influenced by the Italian Renaissance.

Start in the room on your right as you go in. Here you will find a wonderful carved iconostasis by Angelos Mosketis (1683). This was rescued from the church of Pandokrátora (1517), and alongside are photos of the damage to the church caused by the earthquake, and of its reconstruction. The other impressive iconostasis at the end of the room dates from 1690 and is from Agíou Dimítrios tou Kóla (both churches are in Zákynthos Town). There is also a splendid icon of the Virgin from the same church.

As you climb the stairs to the first floor there is a room off to the left, full of icons. A number of these, on the right, came from the old museum. There are some very fine Venetian-inspired paintings from Agías Ekaterínis tou Grypári in Zákynthos Town, and 16th-century icons from Agíou Pnévmatos in Gaïtáni. Perhaps the most interesting work here is the 17th-century representation of Jerusalem from Agías Ekaterínis ton Kípon, Zákynthos Town. Look closely and you will see that this is a very Christian representation of the holy city, with no evidence of its Muslim heritage to be seen.

On the first floor you begin in a small room which contains carved Byzantine stonework (10th- to 11th-century), one piece of which shows the Byzantine double-headed eagle.

Then you enter what is possibly the museum's star exhibit, the fabulous, fully frescoed interior of the monastery church of Agíou Andréa in Mesovoúni Volimón. The church itself is 16th century, while the paintings date from the 17th century. The frescoed interior is set out as it was in situ, and a number of precious sacred vessels are laid out in front of the apse.

There follows a long corridor with a display of silver censers. The first bay contains rescued frescoes from Agíou Georgíou ton Kalogrión (1669); there are also two panels, one of St Nicholas and one of two angels with a scroll, from Agías Ánnas (1715). The second bay has a superb series of icons rescued from across the island. Particularly notable are the Panagía i Amólyndos from Agíou Nikólaou tou Mólou, the 17th-century Ágios Ioánnis o Hrysóstomos from Agíou Ioánni tou Tráfou, and the 17th-century Ascension of the Virgin from the old museum.

Zákynthos Town harbourfront

The next bay holds late 17th- to 18th-century icons, including a splendid 18th-century one of Jonah and the Whale from Agíou Spyrídona tou Flabouriári. The final bay is given over to 12 baroque paintings from the iconostasis of Agíon Anargýron by Nikolaos Koutouzis (1741–1813) and Nikolaos Kantounis (1767–1834). On the way down the stairs, on the left, are Kantounis' paintings from Agíou Georgíou ton Kalogrión.

The final room, on the ground floor, houses a notable model of Zákynthos Town before the 1953 earthquake, giving a good idea of its attractive Italianate character before it was destroyed. On the walls are paintings by Koutzouzis from the church of Agíou Spyrídona tou Flabouriári.

A 17th-century Ionian School icon in the Zákynthos Museum

The Library

Next to the town's theatre, also on Platía Solomoú, is the **Library** (open daily 8.30am–1pm), where there is a small display of photographs showing the island pre-1953. As well as views of the town and the lavish interiors of some of the island's churches, there are photos of the elegant interiors of the mansions of the Zakynthian Italian aristocracy, in particular those of the now-destroyed town palace of the locally prominent Komoutou family. At the top of the stairs is a small room with a rather bizarre collection of dolls in what purports to be traditional Zakyn-thian dress (strictly speaking there is no such thing).

Close to the Library, on the corner of the square by the sea, is the reconstructed church of **Agíou Nikólaou tou Mólou**. The attractive stone building is worth a quick visit. However, many of its original icons are now housed in the nearby Museum of Post-Byzantine Art.

The Solomos Museum

Set back from Platía Solomoú is Platía Agíou Márkou, with a number of cafés, on the far side of which is the **Museum of Dionysios Solomos and Eminent Zakynthians** (open daily 9am–2pm; entrance fee). Named after Greece's national poet, the musem is dedicated to famous Zakynthians – these are noticeably male, and, in most cases, famous in local terms only. Inside, on the left, are the rather grand tombs of Solomos and Andreas Kalvos, a fellow poet *(see box below)*.

The main body of the museum lies upstairs. The room in front of you is dedicated to the fine icon collection of Niko-laos and Thaleia Kolyvos. On the right is a room containing set and costume designs for productions of the work of the playwright Dionysios Romas. The gallery given over to ex-hibits on Solomos himself (writer of the lyrics of the Greek national anthem and a champion of Demotic Greek) has a number of portraits, samples of his handwriting and, more bizarrely, a glass urn contain-ing earth from his first grave in Corfu. Visitors might be surprised to notice that many of the manuscripts are in Ital-ian, his first language. It was only with his rising national-ist conciousness that he turned to writing in Greek.

> In 1960 the bodies of Andreas Kalvos and his English wife were brought to Zákynthos from Keddington, in Lincolnshire, where the poet had spent much of his life.

Further on, there is an interesting case containing memorabilia of the operetta composer and musician Pavlos Karreri (1829–96), otherwise known as Paul Carrer. Close by, there is an imposing coloured lithograph of *The Great Battle of 'Garibaldin' at Siatista under the Leadership of Alexandros Romas'*, next to which is a portrait of Romas himself, looking disturbingly like Joseph Stalin.

Moní Agíou Dionysíou

On the seafront, at the southern end of the harbour, is the most important church of Zákynthos town, **Agíou Dionysíou** (open daily 7am–1pm, 4.30–10pm). It was founded by monks living in seclusion on one of the islands of Strofádes (80km/50 miles south of Zákynthos), where they had been guarding the body of the Zakynthian Ágios Dionýsios. In 1717, to escape the attacks of pirates, they brought the body to Zákynthos and re-established their monastery. In 1764 the church was remodelled, and a bell tower built beside it in 1854. However, the church was completely destroyed in an earthquake in 1893. The present church – an earthquake-proof building – was completed in 1948 and was one of the very few buildings to survive the 1953 earthquake.

The church's interior, although modern, is well worth a look. Every inch is covered with paintings and gilding. Around the church, over the tops of the pillars, are a series of panels describing the exploits of the saint, and of the relic of his body. One of the more bizarre episodes shows the monks using the dessicated body of the saint to expel a plague of locusts. On the right-hand side of the nave is a small chapel containing the grave of the saint. The impressive silver coffin was made in 1829 by Diamantis Bafas. He also made the silver surrounds for the icons on the church's intricately carved wooden iconostasis. The saint has two festival days, celebrated on 24 August and 17 December.

The Froúrio walls

The Bóhali

Above the town in the Bóhali district, is the huge Venetian **Froúrio**, or fort (open daily 8am–2pm; entrance fee). Thought to stand on the site of ancient Psophida, the fortress has Byzantine antecedents, but any traces of these earlier settlements – with the exception of the 12th-century church of the Pandokrátor – have been destroyed by earthquakes. The present fortifications were built under the Venetian *Proveditor general da mar* Giovanni Battisto Grimani and finished in 1646. As a prime defensive site, the fort served as a place of refuge for local people and, particularly in the 17th century, became a flourishing settlement. The fort fell into disuse in 1864, when Zákynthos became part of the Greek Republic.

The Froúrio lies at the end of a winding road that leads up from the town through Bóhali village. Just before the top of the hill is the village *platía* in front of the church, with a few cafés and *tavérnes* that have a lovely view over Zákynthos

Town and harbour. The inside of the fort is now a beautiful pine wood, and you have to search around for the remains of the buildings (there is a useful site plan at the entrance). However, perhaps the main reason for coming up to the Froúrio is the spectacular panoramic view. The site is undergoing a slow renovation by the EU and Greek Ministry of Culture and on the western – sunset – side a café is being built with a superb view of the mountains and plain.

On the way up Bóhali hill, on the left-hand side coming from town, is the **Zákynthos Nautical Museum** (open daily 9.30am–2.30pm, 6.30pm–10.30pm; entrance fee). The work of one man, the museum tells the history of Greek seafaring through a series of model boats, as well as an eclectic assortment of naval artefacts.

Sonnet – To Zante

Fair isle, that from the fairest of all flowers,
Thy gentlest of all gentle names dost take!
How many memories of what radiant hours
At sight of thee and thine at once awake!
How many scenes of what departed bliss!
How many thoughts of what entombéd hopes!
How many visions of a maiden that is
No more – no more upon thy verdant slopes!
No more! Alas, that magical sad sound
Transforming all! Thy charms shall please no more –
Thy memory no more! Acccurséd ground
Henceforth I hold thy flower-enamelled shore,
O hyacinthine isle! O purple Zante!
'Isola d'oro! Fior di Levante!'

Edgar Allan Poe, 1837

THE CENTRAL PLAIN

The island's central plain is
the most fertile in the Ionian
Islands. It is mostly given
over to the intensive cultivation of vines and, away from
the resorts and airport, is
sprinkled with attractive little villages. Separating the
plain from the eastern coast
is a line of steep but low
hills, and on the western
side the mountains rise
sharply and dramatically.
Along the foot of mountains
lie a string of villages, many

**The church tower of Agías
Mávras, Maherádo**

located at points where springs emerge from the hills above.

The central villages include sleepy little Gaïtáni with an
attractive Italianate church, and a characteristic separate bell
tower, which dates from 1906. Similar architecture can be
seen in neighbouring tiny settlements of Vanáto and
Hourhoulídi. The detached bell towers seen across the island
are built away from the church to prevent the bells falling
through its roof in the event of an earthquake.

On the road between Zákynthos Town and Maherádo *(see
page 34)* is the **Ktíma Agría Komoútou** (open daily 9am–
1pm, 5pm–8pm). There has been a vineyard belonging to the
Komoutou family on this spot since 1638, but it was the present owner's father who established the commercial winery,
which now produces some of the best wines on the island.
You can watch the production of the wines, as well as taste
and buy them. Much of the cultivation is organic, and there
is also good olive oil for sale.

Maherádo, Agía Marína and Pigadákia

At the foot of the steep climb up to Kiliómeno is the large village of **Maherádo**, home to a couple of interesting churches and some surviving, albeit decaying, examples of traditional pre-earthquake architecture. The village square by the church of Agías Mávras has two nearby cafés serving basic food such as *souvláki*, salad and *tzatzíki*.

The main sight in Maherádo is the pilgrimage church of **Agías Mávras**. Its baroque interior by Nikolaos Latsis is one of the finest on Zákynthos, and it is said that the church's bells can be heard all over the island. Agía Mávra – whose icon was supposedly found on this spot and the church built around it – is said to help healing, and her silver-framed icon in the centre of the church is hung with many *támata* (votive offerings). Her festival is celebrated at the beginning of June.

On the left-hand side, just after turning up the hill towards Kiliómeno, is a modern convent whose church has an attractively painted interior. Wrap-around skirts are provided for visitors whose dress is not modest enough for a church visit.

North of Maherádo, and higher up the mountainside, is the village of **Agía Marína**. The eponymous church has an

A caper (*káppari*) flower

impressive interior but is often locked. Also here is the **Hélmi Museum of Natural History** (open daily, 9am–2pm Nov–Apr, 9am–6pm May–Oct; entrance fee), with a small but informative display on the flora and fauna of the island.

Further on is **Pigadákia**, named after its springs (*pigí* in Greek). The lovely 16th-century church of **Agíou**

Pandelímona has a holy spring in the saint's shrine under the altar, said to promote healing; this is one of the few places where you can go behind the iconostasis. The traditional *papadosiakoús* dance is performed at the saint's festival on 27 July. The **Vertzagio Museum** (open daily 9am–9pm; entrance fee) here has a somewhat disorganised display of rural artefacts.

Skaliá Cultural Centre

Skaliá Cultural Centre

Three pretty hilltop villages sit on the collines in the north of the plain. They are **Gerakári**, **Kypséli** and **Tragáki**, the southernmost, largest and most strung out. They all give splendid views over the plain below. One of the few places to eat, with basic food, is Harry's *kafenío* and *psistaría* in Tragáki.

Just north of tiny Limodaíka (near Tragáki) is the **Skaliá Cultural Centre/Théatro Avoúri** (tel: 26950 62973). Established by local actor and storyteller Dimitris Avouris in 1995, the beautiful site has three stone-built outdoor theatres, which hold from 60 to 1,000 people, as well as a new indoor auditorium. There are storytelling performances four times a week and, as well as holding Greek and pan-European storytelling festivals, the theatre played its part in the 2004 Cultural Olympiad by hosting global storytelling events. There is also a lovely restaurant *(see page 137)*.

The East Coast

Leaving Zákynthos Town heading north, you pass through **Kryonéri**, along the seafront. The water is reasonably clean, especially given its proximity to the harbour, and the locals swim off the rocks and narrow pebbly beach here. After the steep climb up to pleasant, strung-out Akrotírio, the road runs inland along the ridge before descending back down to the sea at **Tsiliví**.

This is the first of a string of resorts, and not the most pleasant. Situated on a lovely bay with a decent beach, Tsiliví is unfortunately dominated by loud bars, shops peddling tourist souvenirs and holidaymakers going red in the sun. Tsiliví blends seamlessly into Plános before things quieten down a bit at Boúka.

After the small promentory of Akrotírio Gáidaros, for the next 4km (2½ miles) between Aboúla and Amoúdi, the road

A watersports jetty at Alykés

passes turn-offs to a string of small, quiet beaches. There are rooms to rent at most of them, and there are a couple of excellent beachside *tavérnes (see pages 135–7)*. About 1km (½ mile) beyond Amoúdi is **Alikaná**, perhaps the most pleasant of the resorts along this coast. Towards the sea it is still fairly quiet and the mountain backdrop is lovely.

At the northernmost point of the Central Plain is the large resort of **Alykés**. A larger version of Tsiliví, Alykés has all the facilities expected of a Greek package resort – cheap accommodation, all-day English breakfasts and football on satellite TV. It is, however, on a sweeping bay with a sandy beach and views of Kefalloniá. The exposed bay attracts windsurfers and can produce some surf. This is also one of places you can take a boat to the Blue Caves near Skinári (trips are advertised everywhere; *see page 47*). Behind the town are the old saltworks, the large pans forming shallow lakes where salt was obtained from seawater through evaporation. These are now no longer used, as it is cheaper to import salt from the mainland, and the stagnant water can be rather smelly.

LAGANÁS BAY

If you dislike mass tourism and loud nightclubs, the place you will most want to avoid on Zákynthos is Laganás. Ironically, this, the island's most notorious resort, is right in the middle of its most environmentally sensitive area. It is estimated that Zákynthos receives 700,000 visitors every year, half of whom stay in Laganás on the south coast. They come for the wonderful sandy beach that stretches from the Vasilikós Peninsula in the east to Paralía Kerí in the west. However, this stretch of beach is the most important nesting site for the loggerhead turtle *(Caretta caretta)* in the Mediterranean basin. The turtles are very sensitive to human disturbance and have suffered greatly from the indiscriminate development of this coast.

The turtles roam throughout the Mediterranean (there is evidence to suggest they use the Gulf of Gabés off Tunisia as a wintering ground) and in the spring return to Laganás Bay to nest. They rest and mate in the bay while waiting to come ashore during the night. After nightfall, the females crawl up the beach to find a suitable nesting site in the soft sand; if they are disturbed by noises or lights they will return to the sea without laying any eggs. If they are not disturbed, they dig a deep hole and lay a clutch of about 120 eggs. These take about two months to hatch, after which the hatchlings dig their way to surface and – during the night – make their way down to the sea.

National Park Rules

Within the confines of the National Park, you must not:

- fish
- light a fire
- camp
- pick any plants
- throw away ANY rubbish

On the nesting beaches there is:

- no access between 7pm and 7am
- no use of umbrellas 5m (16ft) from the waterline
- no digging in the sand
- no disturbing the cages protecting the nests
- no use of any vehicle
- no access to horses
- no access to dogs without a leash
- no use of ANY lights at night

Access and speed is restricted for boats across the whole area. The strictly protected area around Sekánia has access only for scientists with permission.

Conflicts with humans arise not only due to pressures of space, forcing the turtles on to fewer beaches and raising the nesting density, but particularly due to disturbance of the nests themselves and, once the turtles have emerged from their shells, from light pollution. The hatchlings find their way to the sea using reflected starlight on the

The National Park logo

water. Any shoreside lighting confuses the tiny turtles, causing them to make their way inland, where they die.

National Marine Park

In response to these conflicting demands on the bay – and after intense campaigning by local environmentalists – in 1999 the Greek government established the **National Marine Park of Zákynthos**, the country's first. The protected area, patrolled by 20 park rangers, takes in: the marine area and beaches of Laganás Bay, and around capes Marathiá and Yérakas at either end; a protected area of land stretching back from the beach, and behind that a buffer zone that extends almost as far as Zákynthos Town; and the Strofádes Islands 80km (50 miles) to the south.

The park is home not only to the famous turtles but also the critically endangered Mediterranean monk seal (11–12 of which inhabit sea caves outside of the park), and is important as a rest stop for migrating birds. It also protects certain species of plants, particularly the sea daffodil *(Pancratium maritimum)* and the seabed cover of Posidonia *(Posidonia oceania)*, which contributes a large part of the oxygen in the

Mediterranean. The habitat of **Lake Kerí** is the last remaining wetland of Zákynthos, important for migrating bird species. There used to be a huge lake behind Laganás that stretched almost as far as Zákynthos Town, but this was drained in an act of environmental vandalism to make way for the airport.

The Vasilikós Peninsula

On the eastern side of Laganás Bay is one of the most beautiful parts of the island, the **Vasilikós Peninsula**. Heading south from Zákynthos Town the first place you come to is the resort of Argási. The headquarters of the national park are beside the church here, but there is little else of note. As the land starts to rise, things begin to improve. Set against the backdrop of Mount Skopós, there are a string of beautiful small beaches along the northern edge of the peninsula. The longest of these, Paralía Iónio, is near the strung-out village of

Pórto Zóro on the Vasilikós Peninsula

Vasilikós. Iónio runs into the nudist Banana Beach, and around the cape from here is the popular watersports centre at **Ágios Nikoláos**. On the opposite side of the bay is the unsympathetic development at Pórto Róma.

The best beach, however, is on the southwestern side at **Gérakas**, a superb sweep of sand fringed by cliffs. There is only one problem – this

The crowded beach at Laganás

corner of paradise is an important nesting site for turtles. Access is controlled by a park ranger en route to the beach, and numbers are limited to protect the nests. For those who want to get even closer to nature, the far end of the beach is nudist.

The exemplary **Gérakas Information Centre**, run by the environmental organisation Earth, Sea and Sky, provides information on the turtles and the other flora and fauna of the peninsula. They can also advise on joining volunteer environmental protection programmes (*see page 125*).

Further down the coast is the isolated beach of Dáfni, with a pleasant *psarotavérna*, reached by a very rough road from Vasilikós. Between Dáfni and the beach at **Kalamáki** – perhaps the most pleasant of the hectic resorts on this side of the bay – is the totally protected beach of Sekánia (access is only given to scientists with prior permission).

In the middle of the bay's huge beach is the resort of **Laganás**. This lively nightspot – or den of iniquity, depending on your point of view – is brash, noisy and nocturnal. Apart from its crowded beach, the resort's main attraction is its nightlife; one of the more popular spots is on the island of Ágios Sóstis, joined to the shore by a walkway.

The cliffs at Cape Kerí

THE HILL VILLAGES AND WEST COAST

The wild and mountainous west coast is the least-spoilt part of the island, with hillsides covered in bright green *maquis* and small, dry-stone-walled fields. The land falls to the sea in precipitous cliffs, with no easily accessible beaches; one reason why it has so far resisted tourist development. The sea caves at the foot of the cliffs are used for breeding by the very few remaining pairs of Mediterranean monk seals *(Monarchus monarchus)*. This, and the so-far near-pristine environment, are the reasons why environmentalists are lobbying for protected status (like that for Laganás Bay) for this region.

The hill villages retain much of their traditional character and architecture. You will still see many pre-earthquake buildings, though the majority are too dangerous to live in. One factor that has contributed to their preservation is that no-one can use the damaged buildings unless they have the permission of the owning family, which can be problematic.

Kerí and Agalás

On the western side of the southern cape – best crossed by the spectacular but rough road from Marathiá – is the pretty village of **Kerí**. Many of the traditional houses here have been bought up by German and British visitors, giving the village quite a different, and more reserved, character from other places on the island. As well as a 17th-century church, Kerí is known for the *píssa tou Keríou*, or natural tar pools, mentioned by both Herodotus and Pliny. Now dried up, they were previously used for caulking boats. A couple of kilometers down the road is the lighthouse at Cape Kerí.

The minor road north from the village runs through a very attractive wooded valley. It leads to the quiet village of **Agalás**, tucked away in the southwestern part of the island. Next to the church in the centre is the small maritime and natural history museum and art gallery, though, with its erratic opening times you may have to ask around for the key. Further south into the village, at the point where the KTEL buses drop

> One notable feature of the landscape is the ruined stone towers on the tops of the hills. These are the remains of Venetian windmills, previously used for pumping water up from wells.

off and pick up, you'll find a café and *tavérna*. Signposted off from the village are some Venetian wells and the Damiános cave; both down towards the sea.

Kilioméno and Loúha

At the top of the long, steep climb from Maherádo *(see page 34)* is **Kilioméno**. On the right-hand side, just before the road turns for Ágios Léon, is Korfiatos, a wooden balcony with lovely views, where you can have a drink or simple meal. Behind the benches, which seem more Bavarian than Greek, are huge barrels of local wine. As well as the wine there is also excellent local olive oil and thyme honey for sale. Opposite is Kilioméno's rather odd-looking church of Ágios Nikólaos, with its still-unfinished bell tower.

Leaving Kilioméno, the road turns sharp right and leads to the friendly, if a little lacklustre, village of Ágios Léon. Look out for the Venetian windmill converted into a church tower. A road heading inland from here goes up to **Loúha**, one of the highest, and certainly one of the prettiest, settlements on Zákynthos. The domestic architecture of the hill villages differs from that of the rest of the island; plain exteriors hide pretty courtyards, usually full of flowers, with the living quarters set around them. To get a better look at this arrangement pay a visit to Loúha's tiny village shop and post office (opposite the church of Ioánnis Theológos). The courtyard behind, with a 400-year-old floor, has an attractive *tavérna* on the first floor (with the added bonus of excellent toilets). The previously equally attractive village of Gýrio, just beyond Loúha, has been rather spoilt by a breeze-block factory.

The majority of Zákynthos's high mountain villages are controlled by the KKE (Greek communists). The communists have organised collective agricultural cooperatives to help local famers buy machinery, and then harvest and market their produce

Fresh local produce

From Ágios Léon a pretty but winding, and initially very narrow, road leads down to **Limniónas** by the sea. All that is here is a *tavérna* that looks out over a beautiful rocky bay. Beside the *tavérna* a flight of steps leads down to a small bathing platform.

Éxo Hóra to Anafonítria

The main road carries on north to **Éxo Hóra**. At the crossroads at the village centre is a huge olive tree, reputedly the oldest on the island. The crossroads is also the turn-off for **Kabí**, where a large concrete cross glowers down on the sea from a tall headland. The cross commemorates the place where right-wing soldiers threw a group of local communists to their death in the war, or vice versa, depending whose version of the story you believe.

The unspoilt village of **Mariés** lies further north. Local legend claims Mary Magdalen landed here on

Navágio Bay

her way to or from Rome. This accounts for what seems to be a disproportionate number of churches for the village's size, and for its name (derived from María).

Where the road turns east towards the village of Orthoniés, there is a turn left for **Anafonítria**. Ágios Dionýsios was abbot at the 14th-century monastery here from 1578 to his death in 1622. Further on, above the turn for Navágio *(see below)* is the 16th-century monastery of **Ágios Geórgios ton Krimnón**, with its striking round tower.

Navágio Bay

Just beyond Anafonítria is the headland overlooking **Navágio** (or Shipwreck) **Bay**, on which is the most photographed

Traditional architecture in Volímes (see opposite)

beach in the Ionians – a sheltered bay where a rusty freighter lies half-buried in sand. The locals take great exception to the disfigurement of their spectacular beach (it was previously known as Paradise Beach) and decry the fact that the boat is now regarded as a tourist icon – it was scuttled by an unscrupulous captain, allegedly a smuggler, for a fraudulent insurance claim.

However, looking down the sheer cliffs from the small steel viewing platform above is quite spectacular and, for anyone with even a mild distrust of heights, quite stomach churning. Boat trips shuttle sightseers to the beach from **Pórto Vrómi**, below Mariés. The bigger operators are perhaps best avoided for environmental reasons; boats above a certain size are not supposed to land on the beach, but they invariably do.

Back on the main road, heading further north brings you to Volímes (see opposite).

THE NORTH

North of Alykés the landscape becomes more desolate, rugged and deserted. It was this part of the island that felt the strongest tremors of the 1953 earthquake; the epicentre was in the channel between northern Zákynthos and Kefaloniá.

The long climb out of **Katastári** (the largest village on the island) gives views back to Alykés Bay and over to Kefaloniá. After passing the 16th-century Moní Ágios Ioánnis Prodrómou, with an important icon by Theodore Poulakis, you reach the turn-off for Mariés. The road that heads over to the west coast passes through some stunning scenery.

The road along the east coast then plunges down a very steep (10 percent) hill, passing by **Xýngi** *(see box below)* and around a headland with numerous sea caves, to the beach at **Makrýs Gialós**. Here, there is a camping ground, several places to eat and sea caves you can swim into right by the beach. About 0.5km (500 yards) further on is the tiny headland of **Kokkínou**, where you can pick up a *kaïki* (boat) to the Blue Caves and eat overlooking the boats bobbing in the small inlet. Beyond Kokkínou is the turn-off for the two mountain villages of **Volímes**, famous for their honey and textiles, as well as their surviving traditional mountain architecture.

The road hugs the coast from here to the small port of **Ágios Nikólaos**, with ferries to Kefaloniá and boats to the **Blue Caves** by Cape Skinári, the extreme northern tip of the island with a spectacularly located lighthouse. The water in the caves appears bright blue, and the light colours your skin as you swim *(see also page 37)*.

The sulphurous smell that wafts around the coast at the tiny bay of Xýngi – surrounded by steep walls of rock – emanates from a hot spring in one of the nearby sea caves.

KEFALLONIÁ

Dramatic, rugged and mountainous, Kefalloniá is the largest and highest Ionian island, rising to 1,627m (5,338ft) at the summit of Mount Énos. Although, or perhaps because, tourism is a relatively recent phenomenon on the island, sparked off in part by the book and film, *Captain Corelli's Mandolin (see page 67)*, Ke-

falloniá has one of the least-spoilt environments, and some of the best beaches, in the Ionian Islands. The south is dominated by the heights of Mount Énos, bordered on the west by the Livathó Plain. In the west is the quiet Pallikí Peninsula, while the stunning north coast is fringed by dramatic cliffs.

> The 1953 earthquake devastated almost all of Kefalloniá – with the exception of the far north – causing a huge exodus of refugees. Many settled in Australia, Canada and the USA, although recent years have seen a number of families returning to the island.

ARGOSTÓLI

The island's capital, and also its largest town, **Argostóli** was completely destroyed in the 1953 earthquake and has been rebuilt largely with modern concrete buildings. Although it is essentially a port and administrative centre, the town is not entirely devoid of charm. It has a great position on the Argostóli Gulf overlooking the mountains, has a number of interesting museums, and makes a good base for exploring the rest of the island. Life in Argostóli centres around Platia Valliánou (the central square) and the pedestrianised shopping street of Lithóstroto.

Andísamos Bay

The Archaeological Museum

On P. Vergóti, close to the theatre and opposite the beginning of Lithóstroto, is Argostóli's **Archaeological Museum** (open Tues–Sun 8.30am–3pm; entrance fee). Although small – the museum has just three rooms – the finds are well displayed and help to build up a picture of Kefaloniá's ancient history.

The first room has artefacts from the Palaeolithic to Mycenaean periods, and on the left-hand wall are some interesting archive photos (1899–1933) of excavations on the island. The pieces on display range from very early flint hand tools (100,000–40,000 years old), to clay figurines (c.3rd century BC) from the cult centre of the Nymphs at the Drákinas Cave near Póros. The cave had been a settlement from late neolithic times (8,000BC onwards). The final case has finds (mostly *kantharos*, or double-handled pots) from the late-middle Helladic cist (box-shaped) graves (1750–1700BC) and Mycenaean tholos (beehive) tombs at Kokkoláta, southeast of Argostóli.

> One of the most interesting exhibits in Room 2 of the Archaeological Museum is an Egyptian scarab from the reign of Tuthmosis III (1504–1450bc). It was found in a Mycenaean site at Kráni, indicating that there was trade between Kefaloniá and pharonic Egypt.

Room 2 is given over to finds from Mycenaean, or Mycenaean-influenced sites. By now the visitor will have noticed a certain grave and tomb theme to the exhibits. Perhaps the most important finds in this room come from the tholos tomb at Tzannáta near Póros. These include some delicately beaten gold, one piece of which shows the Mycenaean double-axe, clay figurines and an intriguing bronze buckle, indicating the existence of a powerful Mycenaean centre, probably related to Homeric Ithaca. It is thought that this will be vital evidence in pinpointing the exact location of the mythical kingdom.

A 19th-century view of Argostóli by Joseph Cartwright

The third and final room has displays of pieces from the Classical and Roman eras. On the left are a few larger exhibits, including a charming trident and dolphin floor mosaic from the 2nd-century BC sanctuary of Poseidon at Váltsa, on the Pallikí Peninsula. The cases on the right mostly contain pieces from the four ancient cities of Kefalloniá *(see page 13)*. Notable exhibits include an exquisite gold, winged Niké from Menegáta, a marble head of Silenus from Skiniás and a Roman 3rd-century AD bronze male head from Sámi.

The Korgialénios Museum

Up the hill, past the theatre, is the fascinating **Korgialénios Museum and Library** (Ilía Zervoú; open Mon–Sat 9am–2pm; entrance fee). Set up after the 1953 earthquake to house objects salvaged from the wreckage, the museum gives an overview of 19th-century Kefallonian domestic life. One of the refreshing aspects of the museum is its concentration on

A quiet Lithóstroto at dusk

the lives and world of Kefallonian women, albeit mostly of the urban middle class. To this end, the displays start with a case of household linen, as well as items such as kid gloves, silk stockings and hairpins. What follows is an amazing collection of urban women's costume between 1878 and 1910. They are displayed in period interiors, which give an excellent impression of the life of the Kefallonian aristocracy at the end of the 19th century.

For the most part, the dresses are highly elaborate and beautifully made in lace, silk and satin, with appliqué. There is a lovely pair of bridal shoes from 1905, and particularly exquisite is a young girl's ball gown of 1894, with silk tulle and embroidered roses. There are also a great number of accessories, including shawls, fans, parasols and gloves.

The museum also has a good display of photographs of pre-1953 Argostóli. The earliest, from 1904–6 and taken by local photographer N. Trikardos, show it as a neat, provincial town. Some of the later (1930s) pictures were taken by two members of Kosmetatou family *(see opposite)*. More disturbing are the images showing the total devastation of the town after the 1953 earthquake.

Other displays include a room with some rather dark and heavy furniture and portraits of local worthies, a lovely 18th-century carved and painted wooden iconostasis from the church of Agíou Georgíou, and a case with the effects of Dimitrios Korgialenios (died 1861), a member of the secret pro-independence Filikí Etería (Society of Friends). Finally, after a cluttered but cosy reconstruction of a traditional bedroom, there are displays of agricultural implements.

The Foká-Kosmetátou Foundation

Back towards the central *platía*, at the far end of Valliánou, is a beautifully restored neoclassical mansion housing the **Foká-Kosmetátou Foundation** (open Mon–Sat 9.30am–1pm, 7pm–10pm; entrance fee). The foundation, which was established in 1984 from the estates of three brothers, turned their family home into a museum to display their private collections and to publish studies on Kefalloniá; it has also established the Votanókypos Kefaloniás on the outskirts of town *(see page 56)*.

The museum consists of just one room with, on the right, a display of Greek numismatics and, opposite, a number of lithographs of the Ionians and some pieces of furniture that belonged to the family. Of greatest interest are the lithographs by Joseph Cartwright, Edward Lear and Henry Cook, all of whom published volumes of paintings and engravings of the Ionians. Close by is a fine icon of Ágios Vikédios attributed to Theodoros Poulakis. Also look out for the 10 *dráhmes* banknote from the 1890s, cut in half; each half then became worth five *dráhmes*. The small but pretty garden at the back is used to hold temporary exhibitions.

> 'The buildings of Argostóli are handsome, and the town, though not remarkable for its liveliness, possesses many good streets and public edifices.'
>
> Edward Lear, *Views in the Seven Ionian Islands*, 1863

The Drápano Bridge

Lithóstroto and the Drápano Bridge

The main shopping street of Argostóli is the pedestrianised **Lithóstroto**, which runs south from P. Vergóti, the site of the town's theatre. Reconstructed after the 1953 earthquake, during the 19th and early-20th century the theatre, with its, largely Italian opera productions, was the centre of the social life of Argostóli's middle class. Lithóstroto is lined with cafés, rivals to those in the central *platía*, and pricey clothing and shoe shops. About half-way down, on the right-hand side, is the town's Catholic church. Heavily restored following the earthquake, its chief claim to fame is the 14th-century icon of the Panagía Prevezána. Beyond the church is the **Pýrgos Kabánas** (Kabána Tower). This reconstructed late 18th-century Venetian bell tower now houses a pleasant café decorated with pre-earthquake photographs of Argostóli. The café was created by the municipality and is run as part of the ROTA Cooperative, which places people with mental illness in jobs in the community. On offer are a few local specialities, such as *soumáda* and the Kefallonian *amygdalópita* (almond pie).

At the end of the pedestrianised section of Lithóstroto, turn left down towards the harbour. On the left is the town's produce market. Depending on the season it is piled high with all kinds of colourful agricultural produce.

Walking south along the water brings you to the **Drápano Bridge**. This stone-built causeway (soon to be pedestrianised) crosses the shallow Koútavos Lagoon. Built by the British in

1810, it was overseen by Major de Bosset, Commandant of Kefalloniá, a Swiss soldier in the service of the British army. The obelisk in the centre, on a separate platform, has an inscription to the supposed glories of the British Empire.

The Katavóthres

Rizospáston heads north from the central *platía*. On your right you will pass Argostóli's **Filarmonikí Sholí** (Philharmonic School; currently being restored; *see also page 69*), and opposite, on the corner of the next block, the only building to have survived the 1953 earthquake intact. The streets running off to the right will take you down to the harbour.

The *katavóthres* (sea mills) near Argostóli

By the port authority buildings (near where the ferries depart) is Argostóli's helpful **EOT** (tourist information office; *see page 124*). Further along, past the place on the quay where you catch the ferry for Lixoúri, is a line of *estiatória* (restaurants), the best of which is Patsouras *(see page 139)*. Just beyond, on the left, is a small square. On a small patch of grass is the marble base of a Venetian fountain, with carved lions' heads. The column above it is of later (19th-century) provenance.

Continue along the coast, past a couple of very pleasant *tavérnes* and down a pine-

On a short promontory at Cape Ágios Theódoros is a Doric-collonaded lighthouse dating from 1820. It was commissioned by Charles Napier, who was the British Governor of Kefalloniá between 1822 and 1830.

shaded footpath beside the rocks, where local people swim in the evening. After about a kilometer (½ mile), you reach the tip of the cape. The views here over the mountains and the Argostóli Gulf are spectacular. Also here are the **katavóthres**, or sea-mills, which are the product of a bizarre geological phenomenon. Seawater from the gulf disappears down a series of small sinkholes, only to re-emerge in the cave of Melissáni and under the Gulf of Sámi on the opposite side of the island. The water passes through channels cut by subterranean fresh-water streams during the last ice age, when seawater levels were lower. Fresh water filtering down through the limestone hills increases the flow. As the channels widen the now-brackish water slows, before its resurgence.

The current at the Argostóli end was strong enough in the past to drive mills, built by the British to grind grain. After the 1953 earthquake the flow was disrupted and slowed to the gently running channels you see today. The site itself is now in a sorry state. The original mills were destroyed in 1953 and replaced by a now-disused concrete café and fake water wheel. Further on, around the cape, are a series of small bays where you can swim.

Votanókypos Kefaloniás

Leaving town to the south, following Leofóros Georgíou Vergóti, brings you to a fork in the road. The left carries on to Peratáta, the right-hand turn has a signpost to the **Votanókypos Kefaloniás** (Cephalonia Botanica; open Tues–Sat 10am–2pm, 6pm–8pm; entrance fee). Follow the signs and don't be put off by the rough track, as it soon levels out. Bear left at the top of the rise and the site is 50m (160ft) along on your right. Entrance is free with a ticket to the Foká-Kosmetátou Foundation *(see page 53)*, otherwise leave your money in the honesty box in the hut at the entrance.

This botanical garden was established in 2000 in an old olive grove. Its aim is to represent the rich flora of the different environments found on Kefaloniá, as well as seeking to preserve rare and endangered Kefallonian plants. The garden is allied to the Millennium Seed Bank at London's Kew Gardens. The site is beautiful and a world away from the nearby warehouses on the main road. An artificial stream runs through the centre of well laid-out and labelled areas, and, in spring and early summer, it is lovely to see the floor of the remaining olive grove carpeted with flowers, rather than the ploughed-up versions usually seen from the roadside.

The gardens at Votanókypos Kefaloniás

THE LIVATHÓ AND SOUTH COAST

To the south of Argostóli is the **Livathó Plain**, one of the few level areas on the island. Not surprisingly it is largely given over to agriculture. The road out of town bisects the plain, passing the castle of Agíou Georgíou above the villages of Peratáta and Mazarakáta (site of a Mycenaean necropolis), before, dominated by the bulk of Mount Énos to the east, it hugs the southern coast along to the resort of Skála.

Kástro Agíou Georgíou

Towering above the plain is the renovated **Kástro Agíou Georgíou** (open 15 June–31 Oct, daily 8am–2.30pm; entrance fee). The fortress stands on a pine-clad hill, and can be reached by the turn-off for the Robola Wine Cooperative, and then up by Agíou Nikólaou, or via the hairpinned road from Peratáta. Either route brings you up to the Bórgo, the village outside the castle's walls. The view from the top is spectacular, and either the Castle or Memories café/bar is a good place to take it in, particularly if you have just walked up in the heat and are in need of refreshment.

Icon from Moní Agíou Andréou

There has been a fortress on the site since Byzantine times, centred around the church of Agíou Georgíou from which the castle takes its name. In 1185 the island was taken by the Franks, and the fort was controlled by them until 1485. After a brief period of Turkish rule, the castle passed to the Venetians in 1500 following a three-month seige. The fortifications seen today largely date from the period of Venetian occupation. At this time the castle was the centre of the island's administration, but in 1757 the Venetians moved their official headquarters down to Argostóli, heralding the fort's decline. Like all buildings in southern Kefalloniá, the castle suffered great damage in the 1953 earthquake. However, it is well worth a visit for the view and renovated walls.

Back down in Peratáta, just beyond the village, is the turn for **Moní Agíou Andréou** (also confusingly known as **Moní Milapidiás**). The convent is now housed in mod-

Kástro Agíou Georgíou

ern (post-1953) buildings. Opposite these is the old church of Ágios Andréas, home to important 16th- to 18th-century icons by, among others, Immanuel Lambardos and Athanassios Anninos (1713–48). These are now part of the **Ecclesiatical Museum** (open daily 9am–1.30pm, 5pm–8pm; entrance fee). As well as good Ionian School paintings, the well-laid-out museum has reliquaries containing, allegedly, remains of Ágios Andréas, and some fine ecclesiastical vestments.

Lássi and Metaxáta

A low but steep range of hills separates the Livathó Plain and Argostóli from the west coast. This hides some pretty villages, a couple of good wineries and, on the western side, attractive

Platýs Gialós

beaches. From Argostóli take either the main road out towards Lakíthra (then follow the signposts to the airport), or go around the cape via Ágios Theódoros and a number of bays, along a pleasant pine-flanked road. Both routes are walkable and will bring you to Lássi, the closest resort to Argostóli.

By Greek island standards **Lássi** is fairly low-key, although it does get crowded in high season. The star beaches here are **Makrýs** and **Platýs Gialós**, both with fine sand and clean, blue water. The latter has a small island attached to the beach by a short isthmus. The coastal road continues south above cliffs with lovely views. After a couple of kilometres (1¼ miles) is the **Gentilini Winery** (open 1 June–15 Sept, Tues, Thur and Sat 5.30pm–sunset). Owned by the Kosmetatou family, the winery was established in 1984 and specialises in high-quality organic wines, including a fine Robola.

Above Miniá, close to the airport, is the pretty village of Sarláta, topped by a rather Gothic, ivy-clad ruin. There are a

number of rooms and villas to let here. Just along from Sarláta is **Domáta**, with an impressive church and houses
spilling down the hillside. The church of the Panagía here
contains the coffin in which the remains of Patriarch Grig-
oris V were transported from Istanbul to Odessa. It also has
an interesting 19th-century wooden iconostasis.

The next village is **Metaxáta**, chiefly famous as the place
where Byron stayed for four months in 1823 before leaving
for Mesolóngi on the mainland, where he died. A bust of
the poet can be seen in the main square, close to the site of the
house where he stayed (destroyed in 1953). Below Metaxáta
and Domáta is **Kourkoumeláta**, close to the lovely beach of
Ávythos. The attractive village was rebuilt by Andreas
Vergotis after 1953. At **Pesáda**, where ferries leave for
Ágios Nikólaos on Zákynthos *(see page 47)*, is the **Divino
Winery** (open summer, daily 10am–8pm) which produces a
traditional Muscat, made from sun-dried grapes.

Lourdáta to Skála

From the long beach at **Lourdáta**, just past Pesáda, to the
village of Markópoulo there is little apart from **Moní
Theotókou Sisíon**, believed to have been founded by
St Francis of Assisi. The road south from here is fairly bleak,
though towards the coast the land appears more fertile. After
the right turn-off to Skála, the road rises towards **Markópoulo**. The church of the Panagía here is the scene of a
bizarre festival. Between the 6th and 15th of August hun-
dreds of small, harmless snakes appear, said to bring good
luck to the village.

Taking the left-hand turn to Skála takes you first past
Kateliós, and then the long sweep of sand of **Kamínia**.
Before reaching Kateliós you might want to call in at the
Metaxas Wine Estate (open May–Oct, daily 10.30am–6pm)
and taste their excellent Robola. Kateliós is a tiny, laid-back

resort with a lovely sandy beach, on the opposite side of the bay from Kamínia. This is Kefalloniá's most important nesting beach for loggerhead turtles, although fewer nest here than on Zákynthos *(see page 37)*. Visitors should treat this area with respect and follow the national park guidelines *(see page 38)*. In truth it shouldn't be necessary to disturb the turtles as just along the coast is **Skála**, a popular, but relatively tasteful, resort on a huge sandy beach backed by pine-clad hills. Also here, a little inland, are the excavated remains of a Roman villa with some fine, preserved mosaics.

MOUNT ENOS

The highest mountain in the Ionian islands is **Mount Énos**. At 1,627m (5,338ft) it dominates the southern part of Kefalloniá. Also known by its Venetian name of Monte Nero (the black mountain), its upper reaches are covered by the Greek fir *(Abies cephalonica)*, giving the mountain a dark cap. The fir was first identified on the island (hence its Latin name) and the Énos population is particularly important due to its lack of hybridisation. It is generally found at altitudes of between 800 and 1,600m (2,600–5,250ft) and grows up to 30m (100ft) high. It was an important tree to the ancient Greeks, who used it extensively in shipbuilding.

Énos National Park

The indigenous population of firs is now protected by the **Énos National Park**. This takes in the summit of Mount Énos above 1,000m (3,280ft) and the northern flanks of neighbouring Mount Roúdi (also called Gioúpari; 1,124m/ 3,687ft). The two mountains are divided by a high saddle, which is unfortunately rather marred by a NATO radar station bristling with satellite dishes. A minor road runs up to the saddle from the main road between Argostóli and Sámi. From the radar station it is about 2 hours on foot to the summit (marked by further telecommunication towers); if it is not too hazy the views from the top are incomparable.

The turn-off towards Valsamáta will take you to the **Cephalonian Robola Producers Cooperative** at Frangáta  (open daily 8am–3pm, summer 7am–9pm). The Robola grape is cultivated on the high altitude limestone soils found in the region and is used to produce a fine white wine. The cooperative makes two Robola wines, both of which can be tasted in the visitors' centre.

Close to the winery, just beyond Valsamáta, is **Moní Agíou Gerasímou**. Ágios Gerasímos is the patron saint of Kefalloniá, and the convent, founded in the 16th century, is the most important pilgrimage site on the island. The (male) saint founded a female order in 1554 and was beatified in 1622.

Inside the new convent church, consecrated in 1992, is the saint's silver shrine, inside which is the reliquary containing

Goats on the flanks of Mount Énos

> The semi-wild ponies of Mount Énos are descended from animals abandoned after World War II. They initially formed communities of up to 100 animals, but are now highly endangered, numbering only some 12–14 individuals. If you are lucky enough to spot them, be careful to disturb them as little as possible.

his bones; his funeral robes are draped over the shrine. Although the church is new, it still contains many fine original works of art, as well as a staircase that descends to a couple of small chambers, thought to be the saint's sanctuary.

SÁMI AND PÓROS

The road from Argostóli over the flanks of Mount Énos descends past fir-clad slopes to the small port of **Sámi**. Ferries leave from here for the island of Itháki and Pátra, on the mainland. Sámi is a pleasant, quiet town with a few eating places along the harbourfront. This town was the location for much of the filming of *Captain Corelli's Mandolin* in 2000 (see page 67). For the filming, much of Sámi's pre-earthquake architecture was reconstructed, only to be destroyed during the subsequent battle scenes.

Over the headland of Cape Dihália (also known as Mýtikas) is the beautiful white shingle beach of **Andísamos**, also used as a location for the film. Surrounded by steep, *maquis*-clad hills, the deep inlet looks out on the southern coast of Itháki. The clear water is great for swimming; the furthest little bay of the beach is nudist.

The Drongaráti and Melissáni Caves

On the road from Argostóli, about 3km (2 miles) before Sámi, is the turn for the **Drongaráti Cave** (open summer, daily 8am–8pm; entrance fee). The cave was discovered about 300 years ago, after an earthquake opened up the present entrance. A steep series of steps leads down into a cool fissure, at the bottom of which is a concrete viewing platform overlooking the huge chamber. Occasionally used to hold concerts, it has an impressive array of stalactites. Some of these are damaged, broken off by unthinking souvenir hunters, but there is still a huge amount of flowstone left. From the platform you can make your way down on to the floor of the chamber, where you can explore the nooks and crannies. To see the chamber at its best, wait until the tour groups have departed, when you can explore on your own.

Perhaps even more impressive is the cave lake at **Melissáni** (open 1 May–30 Oct, daily 9am–7pm, 1 Nov–30 Apr, Fri–Sun 10am–4pm; entrance fee), north of Sámi. A short artificial tunnel brings you to the edge of a large underground lake, partly open to the sky due to the collapse of the cavern's roof; the sunlight on the deep, clear water turns it an irridescent blue. Visitors are rowed around the lake by waiting boatmen (a small tip is appreciated).

The Drongaráti Cave

The cave was formed between 20,000 and 16,000 years ago, during the last ice age. The roof of the cavern collapsed some 5,000 years ago, the debris from which still lies in the centre of the lake. Perhaps the most fascinating aspect of its geology is that it is the point of resurgence for the water that sinks at the *katavóthres* near

Looking down into the Melissáni cave lake

Argostóli *(see page 56)*, hence the water in the cave is brackish. It enters the lake at its deepest point (32m/104ft) on the left-hand side, and sinks again at the far point of the still covered section of the cave which lies to your right.

It was in the still intact section of the cavern that archaeological finds were made, dating from the 4th–3rd century BC, confirming that the cave had been the site of a cult of Pan and the Nymphs. These are now in Argostóli Archaeological Museum *(see page 50)*.

From the cave, near Karavómylos, the coast road runs north around the bay of Sámi, to the small port of **Agía Evfimía**. This attractive yachting harbour has a great location, with steep, bare mountainsides looming behind and a sweeping view over the bay to Itháki. The town's narrow shingle beach, north of the yachting harbour – now backed by rather brutal concrete sea walls – has wonderfully clear water, and the swimming here is excellent.

Póros

The main road south from Sámi passes through some beautiful countryside, as well as the attractive mountain villages of Digaléto and Ágios Nikólaos, which are close to the **Ávythos Lake** *(see picture on next page)*. Just beyond Ágios Nikólaos, on the hairpin bends, are the ruins of a monastery. From here the road runs staight down to the village of Tzanáta.

Captain Corelli's Mandolin

This novel, by the British author Louis de Bernières and set in Kefalloniá during World War II, was first published in 1994 and became a bestseller through word of mouth. The book concerns the exploits of Antonio Corelli, a mandolin-playing captain in the occupying Italian army, and Pelagia, daughter of the local doctor. The core of the text is a love story, but this is also set against the German invasion of 1943, after the capitulation of the Italians, and the subsequent massacre of Italian troops, and any islander found helping them, by the German army. Add in the Greek communist resistance, a ridiculous upper-class English intelligence officer who can only speak ancient Greek, and a film tie-in starring Nicolas Cage and Penélope Cruz, shot on location on Kefalloniá, and you have the Captain Corelli phenomenon.

Although the book has been an international success with the reading public (despite being famously slow to get into), it has stirred up the passions of locals and historians alike. Their major objection is the book's portrayal of the communist resistance (known by the acronym ELAS). Well loved and regarded as national heroes by many Greeks – and aided in this case by Italian fighters – its portrayal in the book is suspect. The strong anti-communist – and historically inaccurate – bias to the text slanders not only the movement as a whole, but, more specifically, a surviving partisan, Amos Pampaloni, on whose life it seems to have been based, and who objected strongly to this historical mistreatment.

Tzanáta lies in a fertile bowl. On a small rise in the vale is a Mycenaean tholos (beehive) tomb, excavated in 1992–4. The earliest finds date from c.1350BC, and the high quality of the artefacts – including jewellery, pottery and seals – points to the existence of a powerful Mycenaean centre. It is thought that this may identify Tzanáta as the location of Homeric Ithaca.

Between Tzanáta and Póros the road passes through the short but impressive 80-m (260-ft) deep **Póros Gorge**, the channel for a seasonal river. The town of **Póros** is divided by a rocky headland, on the far side of which is the port and fishing harbour. Ferries sail from here to Kyllíni on the mainland. The Remetzo café/bar at the foot of the jetty is pleasant and also has surprisingly good toilets. As a resort, Póros has a quiet, pleasantly run-down air. The 2-km (1½-mile) long pebbly town beach has very clear water, and there are some secluded rocky bays around the headland.

The Ávythos Lake between Póros and Sámi

To the north of town is the long beach of Rágia, above which is **Moní Theotókou Átrou** (take the right turn just after the gorge on leaving town). This is said to be the oldest monastery on Kefalloniá, first mentioned in 1264. The beautiful road south to Skála runs along the deserted coastline. Before reaching Skála, at Ágios Geórgios, there are the (minimal) remains of a classical temple to Apollo.

THE PALLIKÍ PENINSULA

On the opposite (western) side of the gulf from Argostóli is the large Pallikí Peninsula, which, away from its south coast, is untouched by tourism. On the southeast coast is its major town, and Argostóli's traditional rival, Lixoúri.

Lixoúri

Easily reached by an hourly ferry (around 20 minutes), **Lixoúri** now plays second fiddle to Argostóli and is a sleepy, laid-back place. However, it's worth taking the ferry for the views of the gulf alone, and there are a number of sights worth seeing in the town. It is also a good jumping off point for other places on the peninsula.

Lixoúri developed under Venetian rule (becoming officially recognised in 1534), but about 1.5km (1 mile) north of town is the site of ancient Pali, one of the four ancient city states of the island *(see page 13)*. Much of Lixoúri was destroyed in 1953, but a few major buildings have been reconstructed as before. The earliest of these is the collonaded Markáto, just behind the seafront where the Argostóli ferry docks. It was built in 1824 by the British governor, Charles Napier, and was Kefalloniá's first courtroom.

Further along, on Grígoris Labráki, is the **Filarmoníki Sholí Pállis** (Philharmonic School), in a fine neoclassical building dated 1836 (rebuilt in 1963). There are four such 'schools' – wind and brass ensembles, a legacy of British rule – on the island: here, in Argostóli *(see page 55)*, and in Sámi and Póros. Wind instruments including the flute of founder, Petros Skarlatos (1820–1904), are on show in the prettily decorated first-floor rehearsal room.

Also in the town, up the hill on Ekaterínis (from the port walk up Pávlou Dellapórta, then Mihaïl Avílhou) is the **Lixoúri Museum and Library** (open Tues–Sat 9.30am–1pm; entrance fee). Set in an attractive 1866 neoclassical building with a shady garden, the library holds around 25,000 volumes. The attached museum has three early gospels, as well as 18th- and 19th-century ecclesiastical vestments.

On the waterfront is a statue of local satirical writer and poet Andreas Laskaratos (1811–1901), his back turned on Argostóli across the water. The early nationalist writer Elias Miniates (1669–1714) was also born here.

The South and East Coasts

To the south is the plain of Katogís, the most fertile area on the island, planted with wheat and vines. This suffered greatly in the 1953 earthquake and the effect on the now-fractured topography is obvious. The southern coast has some lovely beaches, and the most popular and spectacular are the red sand stretches of **Mégas Lákkos** and its continuation, **Xí**.

> **Just along from Xí beach, close to Cape Akrotíri, is the Kounópetra (the name literally means, 'rocking stone'). This flat slab of stone used to rock in the waves, but the 1953 earthquake disturbed its balance, so that it no longer moves.**

North of Xí is the village of Madzavináta, unremarkable except for the **Vitoratos Winery** (open summer, daily 10am–2pm and 6pm–8pm). Beyond Madzanináta is **Havriáta**. As well as the church of **Iperagías Theotókou**, it is the location of the school of Vikentiou Damodou (1700–52), one of the

Xí Beach

first on the island. Back towards Lixoúri is **Soullári**, with its church of Agías Marínas, dating from 1600 and containing icons by the Cretan painters Immanuel Moskos and Theodoros Poulakis. The water dripping down in the cave at Moní Agías Paraskevís, by the beach at **Lépeda**, allegedly cures eye infections.

North of town, past the port of ancient Pali at Karavostási, is the monastery of the Panagías at **Kehriónos**; a festival is held here on 23 August. Opposite is the **Sclavos Winery** (open daily in summer, 7pm–9pm). Some 5km (3 miles) further on is a small but important wetland area near the village of **Livádi**.

Anogí

The northern and western mountainous part of the peninsula is known as Anogí. At the southern end of the wild and deserted west coast is the monastery of **Theotókou Kipouríon**, founded in 1759. Perched high on the cliffs, this can be a

spectacular place to watch the sunset. Below is the sea cave of **Drakospilía** (dragon's cave). There is a spring at the nearby ruined church of Agía Paraskeví that is said to cure stomach ailments. Some 10km (6 miles) up the coast – longer by the winding roads – is perhaps the finest beach on the peninsula, **Petaní**, a beautiful stretch of pebbles backed by steep cliffs.

Before reaching Petaní you pass through the village of **Kodogenáda**. In addition to its restored 18th- and 19th-century vernacular architecture, the village is home to two important churches, the 12th- to 13th-century Agíou Georgíou and Agíou Ioánni tou Theológou, with its impressive carved iconostasis.

THE NORTH

The north of Kefalloniá escaped the worst of the ravages of the 1953 earthquake and so has much surviving traditional architecture. The landscape is barren and spectacularly steep, particularly along the precipitous **west coast road**, ◀ which is the best, if most alarming, ride on the island.

Northwest Coast Villages

From Argostóli the road takes you past the turning for the village of **Davgáta**, the location of the **Museum of Natural History** (open Mon–Sat 9am–1pm, 6pm–8pm, Sun 9am–1pm; entrance fee). Set up as an educational centre and library, it provides a useful introduction to the local geology, flora and fauna.

The coast road continues to Fársa, where it starts to climb. Above is the old village, ruined in 1953. Below, and along this whole stretch of coast, you can see rows of fish farms. Beyond Angónas the view along the northwest coast opens up – a steep line of cliffs falling into blue sea. Down to the west are the beaches of **Agías Kyriakís** and **Voúti**. The long, exposed stretch of sand at Agías Kyriakís can attract flotsam, but the small bay at Voúti, down a rough unmade road from the village of Zóla, is cleaner. Although the water isn't the island's clearest, it can get very warm here, even in early summer.

Above: Fabulous view from the west coast road, north Kefalloniá

From here onward the sharp hairpins of the road hug the cliff edges. This is Kefalloniá's equivalent of the oceanside Highway 1 in California. The views – back to the largely inaccessible north coast of Pallikí, and forward to Ásos – are wonderful.

Mýrtos and Ásos

Some 10km (6 miles) beyond Angónas the road turns sharply inland, forming a large hairpin around the truly spectacular bay of **Mýrtos**. The best place to see the beach and cliffs is from the lay-by on the main road on the northern side of the bay. Looking down, you see a crescent of bright white beach bordered by the cornflower blue of the sea and surrounded by sheer cliffs. The way down to the beach is via the steep, but well-paved, road from Divaráta. Once there, it does not quite live up to its view from above. What appeared to be white sand turns out to be small pebbles, and it can get very busy. The beach also feels too organised, with sunbeds, a café and life-guards – essential as the sea can be dangerous here.

> Dating from the late 16th century, the fortress at Ásos was used as a prison until 1953. The prisoners tended the vines that covered the hillsides and clifftops above Ásos village.

From Divaráta the road continues east (turn left before the village to go north). The road crosses the island, through a gap in the mountains, to Agía Evfimía *(see page 66)*, passing on the way a couple of now derelict Venetian windmills that were previously used for pumping water up from wells.

The road north carries on in a similarly spectacular fashion. About 3km (2 miles) after a viewpoint lay-by is the steep descent to **Ásos**. At the bottom is Ásos village, with its charming natural harbour. The village retains much of its traditional architecture (reconstructed with the help of the City of Paris, commemorated by a plaque in Platía Parísion), and in spring and early summer is covered in flowers. The small beach in the harbour is fairly clean, but just round the coast are some beautiful beaches, only accessible by boat.

Connected to the village by a short isthmus is an enormous Venetian *kástro* (fort) on top of a hill. Begun in 1593, it served to protect the Venetian fleet and island from attack by the Ottomans and pirates. In more recent history *(see box, left)* it was used as a prison. The winding path takes you up through pine woods and gives fine views over the harbour and neighbouring coast. Apart from the walls and the lovely curving entrance, little remains inside the fort, although a new visitors' centre has been sensitively built in the middle.

Around Fiskárdo

The road beyond Ásos ends up at the harbour of Fiskárdo at the northeastern tip of the island. This is perhaps the most immediately attractive part of the island, with much surviving traditional venacular architecture. Two of the most attractive **hill villages** here are **Vasilikiádes**, on the main road 10km (6 miles) before Fiskárdo, and **Mesovoúnia**. The latter is on the eastern road to Agía Evfimía. This passes through a string of very pretty mountain villages – **Varý**, **Karyá** and **Komitáta** – and the views over to the neighbouring island of Itháki are

Ásos harbour

magnificent. The only sounds across this landscape, with its dry stone walls and abandoned stone houses, are the tinkling of cow and sheep bells. Water is at a premium here, and there are a number of rainwater cisterns with concrete covered catchments above. The view down to Agía Evfimía from Komitáta is breathtaking.

Towards Fiskárdo itself you pass through **Mánganos**, with its excellent greengrocer (O Manganaras), full of wonderful local fruit and vegetables, and olives, oil and wine, and **Andipáta Erísou**, location of a superb *estiatorío*, To Pevko *(see page 141)*, and the turn-off for Dafnoúdi beach *(see opposite)*. **Fiskárdo** itself survived the 1953 earthquake intact, and has cashed in on this with a vengeance. The admittedly very attractive harbourfront is backed by pastel-shaded housing, now largely expensive restaurants, cafés and boutiques. The harbour, for better or

Fiskárdo waterfront by night

worse, is also greatly beloved by yachties, particularly those on flotilla holidays (it's fun to sit on the quayside watching novice sailors try to bring their boats in for mooring).

The port takes its name from Robert Guiscard, a Norman soldier who died here in 1085, but is thought to be the location of ancient Panormas. There is also a

The beach at Éblisi

Roman cemetery (2nd–4th centuries AD). Towards the Venetian lighthouse, on the northern headland, is an interesting church, started by the Byzantines, but largely Norman in execution (*circa* 12th century). At the southern end of the harbour is the **Fiskárdo Museum** (open daily 10am–5pm). Run by volunteers from the FNEC European exchange programme, it consists of one room with some interesting exhibits, including the skeleton of a Cuvier's beaked whale, found dead on Éblisi beach in 1995, and displays describing local birds and mammals and their habitats.

The northern coast has some wonderful small and quiet **beaches**, all of which have the clearest imaginable water. Some of the little bays, with their white pebble beaches, are only accessible by boat (easily hired for the day in Fiskárdo through a local travel agent). The two most easily accessible from Fiskárdo are, to the north, **Éblisi** and, to the south, the beautiful bay of **Fóki**. Heavenly **Dafnoúdi** is reached by a 20-minute walk down through pine trees from the village of Andipáta Erísou. Tiny **Alatiés**, to the south of Dafnoúdi, could be lovely, but attracts tar (and an unfortunate smell), but nearby **Agía Ierousalím** is a bit cleaner.

ITHÁKI

Easily visited from Kefaloniá, the island of Ithaki has a history that's intimately tied up with that of its larger neighbour. Claimed by many, particularly the locals, to be the mythical homeland of the Homeric hero Odysseus, there is little archaeological evidence to support this claim (indeed, it seems as though Homeric Ithaca is likely to lie close to present-day Póros on Kefaloniá, *see page 68*). Daily ferries leave from Sámi on Kefaloniá and dock at the tiny harbour of Píso Aetós on the west coast of Ithaki.

Like Kefaloniá, Ithaki suffered greatly from the 1953 earthquake, causing many people to emigrate (the population dropped from around 15,000 to under 3,000). However, it is a supremely beautiful and unspoilt island with a lovely main town, Vathý, and some gorgeous deserted beaches.

VATHY AND THE NORTH

Vathý lies on the island's east coast, at the head of a deep bay on the Gulf of Mólou. It is a quiet, very attractive town (it still retains surviving pre-earthquake architecture) with a huge number of *tavérnes* set around its harbourfront and an **Archaeological Museum** (open Tues–Sun 8am–2.30pm; entrance fee). Ferries leave here for Pátra on the mainland.

To the north, the road crosses the isthmus and either heads up to the mountain-top village of Anogí, or around the western coast through Lévki. **Anogí**, only occupied for half the year,

Ithaki is essentially two groups of mountains linked by a narrow isthmus. On the eastern side of the isthmus is the deep Gulf of Mólou, while on the north coast is the large bay of Afáles.

The harbour of Píso Aetós

Itháki's main town, Vathý

has fabulous views as well as the Byzantine church of Kímisis tis Theotókou. Before reaching Lévki you pass a series of small, quiet pebble beaches: Vrýsi, Áspros Gialós, Komninoú Ámmos and Koutoúpi.

The roads from both Lévki and Anogí join at **Stavrós**, the island's second-largest town. This sits above the small port of Pólis (a 20-minute walk). There is a small **Archaeological Museum** (open Tues–Sun 9.30am–2.30pm; entrance fee) here, housing local finds. These mostly come from the early Bronze-Age to Mycenaean site at nearby Pelikáta, one of the many sites claimed as the location of the palace of Odysseus *(see page 79)*.

North of Stavrós a road winds up to the hill village of Exogí. On the way up is an excavation known as the School of Homer, in reality a tower dating from the 6th century BC; close by is Mycenaean tomb. Below is the spectacular bay of **Afáles** with its lovely beach. From the beach at Afáles a rough, but beautiful minor road heads north towards Cape Drákou Pídimia, before doubling back down to the deserted beach at Mármaka.

After the quiet port of Fríkes on the east coast, a favourite yachting harbour, the main road heads around to **Kióni**, an attractive place and Itháki's most upmarket resort. Like Fiskárdo on Kefalloniá, Kióni survived the 1953 earthquake, and has capitalised on this in a similar fashion, as evidenced in the prices for accommodation. The coast between Fríkes and Kióni has a number of lovely pebbly beaches. The walk up to Anogí, from Kióni, along a clearly marked path is delightful and takes around 1½ hours each way.

THE ODYSSEUS TRAIL

The south of the island has a number of sites that are supposedly linked with events in Homer's *The Odyssey (see page 15)*. Close to Vathý, up the hill from the beach at Dexá (identified as ancient Phorcys, the landing place of Odysseus), is the **Cave of the Nymphs**. This spot is apparently where the Greek hero, helped by the goddess Athene, hid the cauldrons, tripods, cloaks and cups given to him by the Phaeacian king, Alcinous.

Odysseus, transformed by the goddess into an old man, met up with Eumaeus (his old palace swineherd) at the **Arethousa Spring**, where the pigs were being watered. The spring is in the south of the island, 3km (2 miles) from Vathý, along a steep but well-marked path. Above the spring is the Cave of Eumaeus.

On the other side of the island, towards the harbour and pebble beach at **Píso Aetós**, is the site of **Alalkomenes** (c.700BC). This was wrongly identified by the German archaeologist Heinrich Schliemann in 1878 as the palace of Odysseus (where the hero came to win back his wife, Penelope, from her suitors).

Above Píso Aetós is the village of **Perahóri**, which is close to the island's now deserted and ruined medieval capital, Paleóhora.

Venetian windmills near Kióni

WHAT TO DO

SPORTS

The wonderfully clear sea and spectacular mountains of Zákynthos and Kefalloniá invite visitors to do more than just sit in a deck chair looking out at the view. Options for active holidays are numerous, from swimming, diving and sailing to walking, cycling and horse riding.

Watersports

Swimming. The water quality around the islands is excellent. The water is extremely clear and clean and, in general, safe; though be careful at some of the west-facing beaches, particularly Mýrtos on Kefalloniá, as there can be nasty undercurrents. For small children, the southern and eastern beaches of Zákynthos (for example Kalamáki, Pórto Koúkla and Tsiliví) are best, as they have gently sloping sand and calm waters. Otherwise, most hotels and apartments have swimming pools, though in summer it would be a shame not take advantage of the warm waters surrounding the islands. At some points (notably the pebbly beaches around the north and eastern coasts of Kefalloniá) the view from the water over to Itháki or Levkáda is stunning.

Hiring a small (25 horse-power) motor boat is the best way to explore secluded and otherwise inaccessible bays. They are available from travel agents in many places (particularly on Kefalloniá) and cost €60–80 per day plus petrol. They are great for swimming from – simply anchor, then dive or jump off the side; all boats have a fold-down ladder to help you get back on board.

Paddling in wonderfully clear water at Marathiá beach, Zákynthos

Snorkelling and diving. The coasts around Zákynthos and Kefaloniá are a divers' paradise – the rocky shoreline is home to wide variety of creatures, and the calm, clear water gives visibility up to 50m (165ft). All scuba-diving schools have qualified instructors who will choose dive locations according to your experience. Extended boat trips are available for advanced divers. For the more advanced trips, or to hire equipment and go by yourself, you will need to show a diving certificate. Most major resorts have reputable diving schools. Well-reputed dive centres approved by the Professional Association of Diving Instructors (PADI; <www.padi.com>) include Divers Paradise at the Louis Zante Beach Hotel (tel: 26950 51130; <www.diversparadise.gr>), on Zákynthos, and Aquatic World in Agía Evfimía (tel: 26740 62006; <www.aquatic.gr>), on Kefaloniá. If you don't want to indulge in full-scale scuba diving, snorkelling with simply a mask, snorkel and flippers can be equally rewarding.

Yachting

The relatively calm and safe waters around Zákynthos and Kefaloniá, coupled with the wonderful marine environment, have made this area very popular with yacht owners and companies running bareboat charter and flotilla holidays. On Kefaloniá the most popular harbour is Fiskárdo in the north of the island. However, this can get very busy, especially with novice crews being instructed through loudhailers by their group leader on the quayside. If you are after a little more peace and quiet then you would be better advised to head down the coast to Agía Evfimía, or along the spectacular west coast to the pretty horseshoe harbour of Ásos. Companies that charter boats and run flotillas include Sunsail <www.sunsail.com> and Templecraft <templecraft.com>. For something a little different, check out <www.nudesailing.co.uk>.

Water sports. Zákynthos is the best island to visit for organised water sports, with major centres located at Tsiliví, Alykés and Ágios Nikólaos in the Vasilikós Peninsula. Boards and sails for windsurfing are available for hire at certain beaches, and instruction is offered at many places. Parasailing, which is now very popular, is available at several beaches on Zákynthos, as is jet-skiing.

A yacht at Cape Skinári, Zákynthos

Walking

The islands not only have wonderful coasts, but also beautiful interiors, much of them mountainous. There is some superb walking here, and not all of it strenuous. The goal of more serious hikers will be the summit of Mount Énos (the highest peak in the Ionians), best tackled from the saddle between it and Mount Roúdi *(see page 62)*. For gentler, self guided, walks log on to the Friends of the Ionian site <www.foi.org.uk> to download very informative walks leaflets (to access this information you will have to join the organisation and make a small donation). There are also companies that conduct walking tours of the islands, for interesting trips to Kefalloniá contact Sea Trek Adventures (tel: 01386 848814; <www.sea-trek.co.uk>). Serious botanists will find the hills of the islands a delight, and there are tailor-made botanical walking holidays available.

Horses at the Bavarian Riding Stables near Sámi, Kefalloniá.

Horse Riding and Cycling

These are both excellent ways of seeing the islands. On Kefalloniá the Bavarian Horse Riding Stables, in Koulouráta about 6km (4 miles) south of Sámi, offers trips from one to seven days on horseback into the mountains and along the coast (tel: 6977 533203; <www.kephalonia.com>). The mountainous nature of the terrain makes cycling hard work, but extremely rewarding. Many of the minor roads are very quiet, but take great care on the precipitous main coast roads.

Excursions by Kaïki

Numerous small boats offer excursions around the islands. Popular trips on Zákynthos are to the Blue Caves at Cape Skinári (take the *kaïki* from Ágios Nikólaos) and to Navágio Beach *(see page 46)*. There are also turtle-spotting trips around Laganás Bay; for the most environmentally sensitive trips contact Earth, Sea and Sky via <www.earthseasky.org>.

Environmental Volunteers

One of the most satisfying ways of seeing the islands is to volunteer on an environmental protection programme run by one of the local eco-groups. On Zákynthos much of the work is dedicated to safeguarding the nesting loggerhead turtles on Laganás Bay and to protecting the environment of the National Marine Park.

Several organisations are involved in this; the park authority itself is setting up a voluntary scheme (see their website <www.nmp-zak.org> for details), but the longest-standing organisations on Zákynthos are the Sea Turtle Protection Society of Greece (<www.archelon.gr>) and Earth, Sea and Sky (<www.earthseasky.org>). Both run turtle protection programmes, while Earth, Sea and Sky organise other activities such as litter collection and fire prevention.

On Kefalloniá, visitors below the age of 25 can apply to FNEC (Fiskárdo's Nautical and Environmental Club; <www.fnec.gr>) to take part in their environmental protection programmes. As well as carrying out marine research work, they also run a network of volunteers to protect the feral ponies of Mount Énos.

SHOPPING

Prices are rising in Greece, and as a result you shouldn't expect great bargains on either Zákynthos or Kefalloniá. In souvenir and gift shops you might find that some good-natured bargaining is tolerated if you are buying more than one item or spending a reasonable amount, but don't push your luck. Local profit margins have to cover not only the tourist months but also the off season, when shops are often closed.

If you are not a resident of the EU, you might be able to claim back the 18 percent VAT (sales tax) included in the price of most goods (if you spend over a certain amount). Ask for details at shops with 'Tax-Free for Tourists' stickers.

What to Buy

Truth be told, Zákynthos and Kefalloniá are not a shoppers' paradise, and the best things to buy as gifts or mementos of your trip are perishables, such as olive oil, thyme honey and local wines *(see page 99)*. Among the tourist merchandise peddled in the resorts, from inflatable turtles and novelty keyrings to mass-produced figurines, you'll have to look hard to find anything worth bringing home. An exception to this is jewellery, in gold and silver, which can be of very good quality and made in attractive, unusual designs. Zákynthos Town is a good place to look: try either Savvas (tel: 26950 29188) or Platinum (tel: 26950 27022), both of which are on Platía Agíou Márkou. In Argostóli most of the jewellers are along Lithóstroto. Note that the more upmarket the resort (for example, Fiskárdo), the more inflated the price of the jewellery is likely to be.

Bottles of olive oil for sale, Kiliómeno, Zákynthos

Another item worth looking out for is a decent reproduction icon. These can be skilfully executed and are widely available, but the best ones tend to be on sale at museums and monasteries.

Leather items, especially bags and sandals, can be good buys, but you might want to shop around for the best quality and selection.

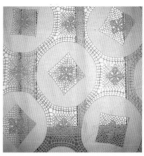
Lace from Volímes, Zákynthos

Ceramics are among the few artisanal items worth bringing home, and the islands have some excellent craft potters, particularly in the attractive smaller villages. You may also consider buying hand-embroidered textiles; the women's cooperative in Volímes, Zákynthos, has an excellent reputation.

NIGHTLIFE

There are considerable differences in the nightlife on the two islands. For the most part, nightlife on Zákynthos falls into two broad types: that which is more traditionally Greek, ranging from the authentic (*kandádes* evenings in *tavérnes; see page 12*) to the heavily tourist-orientated ('Greek nights'; *see page 90*) and that revolving around the clubs in the resorts. If the latter is your thing, then head straight for Laganás on Zákynthos, which has many such establishments (including Rescues, the largest club outside of Athens). Other places to check out include Cherry Bay Beach Club, Zeros and the Cameo Club, which is on the small island of Ágios Sóstis, accessible across a walkway from the beach. Elsewhere on Zákynthos, the clubs in Argási are pretty lively, while those in the resorts of Tsiliví and Alykés are a little more staid.

A more cultural excursion on Zákynthos would be a night-time trip to catch a performance at the Théatro Avoúri in the Skaliá Cultural Centre *(see page 35)*.

Kefalloniá's nightlife is rather more low key and, in Argostóli, revolves around the cafés and bars on Platía Valliánou and Lithóstroto. A pleasant alternative for a night out is to visit the outdoor cinema 'Anny', near the central *platía* opposite the fire station (films start at 9.30pm and are usually Hollywood blockbusters in English with Greek sub-titles). Elsewhere on the island, apart from in the more lively resort of Lássi, nightlife is focused on the local bar, or on going out to eat in a nearby *tavérna*.

Greek Nights

Whichever resort you are staying in on Zákynthos, you will almost certainly come across a 'Greek Night', which generally

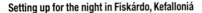

Setting up for the night in Fiskárdo, Kefalloniá

comprises a fairly traditional meal, music (usually live) and dancing. It is, of course, the last that everyone comes to see. Traditional Greek dances are taught at an early age, and the dancers – be they specially hired performers, restaurant staff or simply locals who want to do their bit – can almost always be relied on for an energetic performance.

A lively bar in the resort of Laganás, Zákynthos

Whereas some Greek island dances are a little staid, Zakynthian males revel in athletic, fast dances with high-kicking, Cossack-like steps and not a little bravado. Dancing in a ring of fire is quite typical. Another dance involves picking up a glass of wine with the mouth (no hands allowed) from a press-up position. The wine is downed with a jerk of the neck. Another crowd pleaser is the solo *zeïbékikos*. The spectators, clapping in time to the music, cheer on the dance. By the end of the night, it is a fair bet that the dancers will have cajoled everyone up on to the floor to join in a version of the *syrtáki,* Greece's best-known group dance; the steps are simplified for visitors.

These dances are usually all accompanied by the famous eight-stringed lute, the *bouzoúki,* which for many foreigners has become synonymous with all Greek music. In fact, the instrument (which is of Middle Eastern origin) is a comparatively recent import to the island, though the haunting melodies of Manos Hadjidakis and Mikis Theodorakis have made it an intrinsic part of Greek folklore.

CHILDREN

It is easy to travel with a family in Greece, and Zákynthos in particular is a popular destination for those with children. The Greeks are very tolerant of children – it is common to see local youngsters late at night in *tavérnes*, eating and running around, and visitors' children will be accepted doing the same. In addition, many of the larger and more expensive hotels and resorts have facilities for children, including play areas and dedicated, shallow swimming pools.

Many of the activities already mentioned are suitable for children, and the active, outdoor life should appeal greatly to those with an adventurous spirit, with the beach being the obvious focus of activities. Do remember, however, that the Mediterranean sun is very strong, and that children can burn easily and quickly. Make sure they wear a T-shirt and use a high-factor sunscreen.

On Zákynthos there are two 'toy trains' that might appeal to children. One runs frequently to and from Zákynthos Town to Argási, and another goes from Alykés in a circle through the nearby countryside, passing through Katastári and Pigadákia. Trekking on horseback is also a possibility *(see page 86)*, though this is not one for very young children.

Inflatable turtle, Zákynthos

Activities centred around wildlife can also be popular. Trips to see the turtles *(see page 86)* and visits to the two natural history museums *(see pages 34 and 73)* are possible excursions that will go down well with the kids.

Calendar of Events

1 January New Year's Day *(Protohroniá)*. Feast Day of Ágios Vasílis (St Basil). Before Western ideas of Santa Claus became widespread in Greece, this was the traditional day on which gifts were exchanged. Children go from house to house singing the traditional *kálanda*.

6 January Epiphany *(Agía Theofánia* or *Fóta)*. In seaside parishes the priest or bishop blesses the waters by throwing a crucifix into the sea, then young men dive to retrieve it.

Easter The great festival of the Greek year. A moveable feast comprising several parts: **February**, *Apókries*, the period before Lent that is Greece's carnival season; **Clean Monday**, the first day of Orthodox Lent *(Katharí Devtéra)*, when in good weather everyone goes out for a picnic; **Good Friday**, biers *(epitávia)* from many churches are taken on a procession; **Easter Sunday**, at midnight on the Saturday the priest announces *Hristós Anésti* (Christ has risen) and passes the flame of life from the altar to the candles of the congregation. There then follow fireworks and noisy celebrations with music and dance.

25 March Independence Day.

1 May May Day. Workers' parades and excursions to the countryside to gather flowers and greenery for May wreaths.

3 May Feast of Agía Mávra, Maherádo, Zákynthos.

21 May Ionian Union Day *(Énosis ton Eptaníson)* marks the anniversary of the seven islands joining the modern Greek state in 1864.

15 August Assumption of the Virgin Mary *(Apokímisis tis Panagías)*, celebrated most bizarrely in the village of Markópoulo, Kefalloniá, by a 'snake festival' (6–15 August).

16 August Feast day of Ágios Gerásimos, patron saint of Kefalloniá (also 20 October).

24 August Feast day of Ágios Dionýsios (patron saint of the island), Zákynthos Town (also 17 December).

28 October *Óhi* Day. Celebration of the Greek refusal in 1941 to accept Mussolini's ultimatum, triggering their heroic resistance of Italy's invasion.

25 December Christmas Day.

EATING OUT

In general, Greek food is delicious, fresh and well prepared. Traditionally, a restaurant *(estiatório)* does not have entertainment; it is a place for straightforward eating. These often provide *magirevtá*, oven-cooked dishes that you choose by entering the kitchen and indicating what you want. *Tavérnes*, usually open only at night, and are more social establishments where customers may spend an entire evening drinking and eating; *psarotavérnes* specialise in fish and seafood. A *psistariá* has rotary and flat grills for cooking meats and poultry.

Mezédes and Salads

Mezédes are small plates of food, akin to starters. They can be used in combination to make up whole meals. Common *mezédes* include: olives; *tzatzíki* (yoghurt dip flavoured with garlic, cucumber and mint); *taramosaláta* (fish-roe paste blended with breadcrumbs); *melitzanosaláta* (aubergine salad); *gígandes* (broad beans in tomato sauce); and *dolmádes* (vine leaves stuffed with rice and spices). *Kalamarákia tiganitá* are pieces of deep-fried squid (this is usually frozen, not fresh); *tyropitákia* are small pastry parcels filled with cheese; *keftédes* are small, fried meatballs flavoured with coriander and spices; and *saganáki* is a slice of cheese coated in flour and fried. The standard Greek salad of tomato, cucumber, pepper, olives and feta cheese *(horiátiki saláta)* is a fine staple. *Maroúli* is lettuce, at its best as a finely shredded salad

> Greek food is served lukewarm and with lots of olive oil, thought of as good for the digestion. For hot food, ask for it *zestó*; food without oil is *horís ládi*. However, both these requests will be considered eccentric.

Dining out on Sámi waterfront

with spring onions and dill. Also popular, are various cold or lukewarm salads of boiled wild greens *(hórta)*.

Main Courses

Common dishes include, *mousakás* (minced meat, aubergine and tomato with béchamel sauce and a cheese topping), brought to Greece by refugees from Asia Minor, and *pastítsio* (macaroni and minced meat with béchamel sauce). *Kléftiko* is lamb, slowly baked until it is very tender, and *stifádo* is braised beef with onions. *Briám* (potatoes, tomatoes and courgettes) and *fasolákia laderá* (green beans and tomato sauce) are two other popular casserole dishes, while *fasoláda* (bean soup) is also a favourite. A treat, if you can find them, are *angináres* (artichokes); *bámies* (okra) are also particularly good.

Meats grilled on a small skewer are known as *souvláki*, while *gýros* are thin slices of meat cut from a spit and served

Argostóli's wonderful fruit and vegetable market

with salad on pitta bread. *Biftéki*, fried minced meat mixed with bread and spices, is ubiquitous. *Giouvétsi* is beef or lamb, pasta and tomato cooked in a pot. *Soutzoukákia* are rolls of minced meat cooked in tomato sauce. *Giouvarlákia* are rolls of minced meat covered in egg-and-lemon sauce *(avgolémono)*. For more unusual foods you may encounter *kokorétsi* (lamb's offal wrapped in intestines and grilled over a spit), *myaló* (fried sheep brains), or sheep testicles, known as 'unmentionables' *(amelétita)*. *Pátsa* is tripe, served up in a spicy soup, much vaunted as a hangover cure. If you are in Greece at Easter, try the tasty *magerítsa*, a soup made from finely chopped lamb's offal.

Although desserts are not commonly offered, particularly in traditonal establishments, those you are most likely to encounter include yoghurt with honey, often with walnuts, and two kinds of *halvá. Halvá tis rínas* is a semolina cake and the compact *halvá tou bakáli*, the grocer's *halvá*, is made of flour, tahini, oil, honey and nuts. Sometimes you will find *galaktoboúreko*, filo pastry filled with custard and soaked in syrup, and *baklavás*, made of crushed nuts in filo pastry with syrup. In the summer, particularly late summer, don't miss the abundant grapes, figs, melon and watermelon.

Local Dishes

There are a number of specialities that come from the two islands, some of which bear testimony to their history of invasion and occupation. On Zákynthos there is a strong tradition of home jam-making (known as *marmeláda*, from the English marmelade), although you will be lucky find any outside of private houses. There is much influence from Italy across the Ionians, and this is seen in dishes such as *sofrítto*, lightly fried veal with garlic and vinegar; *bourthíto*, a peppered fish stew; *biánco*, white fish stew with garlic; and *pastitsáda*, a spicy meat, macaroni and cheese dish. *Pandséta*, found on Zákynthos, is very similar to the Italian cured pork *pancetta*.

Kefalloniá has its *kreatópita*, a pie consisting of meat and rice flavoured with cinammon and topped with a thick pastry. This is available almost everywhere, while rather more unusual is the octopus pie traditionally eaten during Lent. You may also come across boiled goats' meat on Kefalloniá.

Psarotavérnes

These can be very expensive, but will have some fresh fish unless winds have kept the boats in harbour. Fresh fish is sold by weight (before it is cleaned) and you might want to keep an eye on the scales, also look out for fish marked *katapsygméno* (frozen), sometimes just 'kat' or 'k'. Fish sizes vary from the tiny whitebait *(marídes)* and smelt *(atherína)*, to the larger dentex *(synagrída)*, swordfish *(xifías)* or grouper *(rofís)*. In between are the smaller red mullet *(barboúni* or *koutsomoúra)* and several breams *(tsipoúra, fangrí, sargós* and *lithríni)*. Cod *(bakaliáros)*, salted or fresh, as well as *galéos*, a kind of shark, is common. Grilled octopus *(htapódi)* and cuttlefish *(soupiá)* are delicious, and deep fried squid *(kalamarákia)*, usually frozen, is often available. You may also find lobster *(astakós)*, usually boiled, but sometimes cooked with spaghetti.

An Ionian quirk is *aliáda*, essentially the same as the garlic purée found elsewhere in Greece (where it is known as *skordaliá*) but made with potatoes rather than bread. Also look out for delicious, local *kolokythákia* (courgettes) boiled whole and served with vinegar. Local cheeses are worth trying anywhere, and those made from sheep's milk are often excellent, though many of the harder ones can be very strong and salty.

Both islands have excellent thyme honey, sold by the wayside in large jars, but this is not the only sweet speciality. Zákynthos produces a very sweet nougat called *mandoláto*, made from almonds and honey. *Amygdalópita* (almond pie) is a speciality of Kefalloniá, where you will also find *kydónopasto*, a quince paste similar to the Spanish *membrillo*.

Barrelled wine, oil and honey in Kilioméno

What to Drink

In the summer you will need to drink a lot of water, but do try to steer clear of bottled 'spring' water, as Greece's mountain of plastic bottles is growing ever higher. Tap water is perfectly safe on both Zákynthos and Kefalloniá, though it is extremely hard. If you carry your own water bottle, cafés and restaurants you visit will be happy to fill it for you.

Better still, find one of the islands' well-regarded springs, from which locals often take their own drinking water.

Greece has delicious bottled fizzy lemonade *(lemonáda)*, which, unlike some other 'lemon drinks', does actually contain lemon juice; the best brands are Loux and IVI (HBH). Another drink worth looking out for is *soumáda*, a diluted orgeat syrup made from barley and almonds. Beer is widely available, the most likely offerings being Amstel and the more palatable Heineken; however, the local brand, Mythos, produced by the Boutari company, is one of the best.

Greece has been making wine for millennia, and, although in the past some of its wines have been particularly esteemed, few are now well known outside the country. Kefalloniá is one of the best wine-producing islands and is particularly noted for whites made from the Robola grape, given an Apellation of Superior Quality. The vines grow well in the dry, stony soils common on the island, and it is possible to visit a number of the best wineries *(see pages 60–3)*. Other major grape varieties include Muscat, used for a very fine sweet wine, and Mavrodaphne, which produces a strong red. Zákynthos also has a few good wines *(see page 33)*, and its own cultivar, Zakynthino.

Local barrelled wines can be surprisingly good and are always worth a try. Resinated wine *(retsína)* can also be good, particularly when served very cold. *Oúzo*, a grape distillate with added aniseed oil, is drunk as an aperitif with water. *Tsípouro* is a clear, fiery grape distillate similar to the Italian *grappa*.

Juicy olives for sale

Freshly baked biscuits in Argostóli

To Help You Order…

Is there a table available, please?
Ypárhi éna trapézi eléfthero, parakaló?

I'd like a/some…
Tha íthela éna, mía/meriká…

The bill, please.
To logariasmó, parakaló.

Basic Foods

aláti	salt	**tyrí**	cheese
avgá	eggs	**voútyro**	butter
kremídia	onions	**xýdi**	vinegar
ládi	(olive) oil	**gaoúrti**	yoghurt
makarónia	pasta	**záhari**	sugar
méli	honey		
pipéri	pepper	***Mezédes***	
psomí	bread	**andzoúyes**	anchovies
rýzi	rice	**dolmádes**	stuffed
skórdo	garlic		vine-leaves

elëés	olives	htapódi	octopus
fáva	split peas	kalamarákia	squid
kolokithákia	fried	katepsigméno	frozen
tiganités	courgettes	marídes	whitebait
loukánika	sausages	mýdia	mussels
melitzánes	fried	psári	fish
tiganités	aubergines	sardéles	sardines
saganáki	fried cheese	soupyés	cuttlefish
spanakópita	spinach pie	xifías	swordfish
taramosaláta	fish-roe dip		
tyropitákia	cheese pies		
tzatzíki	yoghurt	***Fruit and Vegetables***	
	with garlic	angináres	artichokes
		arakádes	peas
		domátes	stuffed
Meat		gemistés	tomatoes
arní	lamb	fasólia	haricot
biftéki	minced meat		beans
	cake	hórta	greens
brizóla	chop	horiátiki	'Greek
hirinó	pork		salad'
keftédes	meatballs	kolokithákia	courgettes
kotópoulo	chicken	karpoúzi	watermelon
kréas	meat	maroúli	lettuce
moshári	veal/beef	lemóni	lemon
sta kárvouna	grilled	patátes	potatoes
sto fúrno	roast	(tiganités/	(chips/
soutzoukákia	meatballs	sto fúrno)	roast)
souvláki	spit-roast	piperyés	stuffed
		yemistés	peppers
		portokáli	orange
Fish		saláta	salad
bakaliáros	salt cod	stavýlia	grapes
barboúnia	red mullet	sýka	figs
frésko	fresh	veríkoka	apricot
garídes	prawns		

HANDY TRAVEL TIPS

An A–Z Summary of Practical Information

A

ACCOMMODATION

Many hotels are heavily booked with package tours from mid-June until mid-September, especially during the first three weeks of August. Reservations are strongly recommended. If you do arrive on Kefalloniá without one, go to the Tourist Information Office in Argostóli *(see Tourist Information on page 124)*. In extreme difficulties, the Tourist Police may be able to help with finding a room.

Prices are controlled according to a rating system, based on a building's age, facilities, amenities and other factors. Hotels are rated from A to E (rooms in categories A and B have private bathrooms), but prices can vary widely within each category. Luxury establishments, rated L, are not price-controlled. A star system, designed to replace the letter scheme, was introduced in 2003, but has met with resistance. The equivalents are roughly as follows:

Luxury – 5 stars
A – 4 stars
B – 3 stars
C – 2 stars
D and E – 1 star.

In high summer some form of air conditioning will enable you to get a good night's sleep. If your room doesn't have air conditioning (and some older properties don't), there will either be a ceiling fan, or you might be able to borrow a fan from reception or the owner.

Villas and Apartments. Zákynthos and Kefalloniá have many villas, apartments and studios (the latter terms are interchangeable) to rent. Accommodation ranges from simple rooms to lavishly appointed summer homes – sometimes tastefully converted from a traditional house or houses – complete with swimming pool. In the

UK, companies specialising in top-of-the-range secluded luxury villas on Zákynthos and Kefalloniá are: Ionian Island Holidays, tel: 020 8459 0777, <www.ionianislandholidays.com>; Simply Ionian, tel: 020 8541 2200, <www.simplytravel.co.uk>; Sunisle, tel: 0871 222 1226, <www.sunisle.co.uk>; Sunvil (Greek Islands Club), tel: 020 8232 9780, <www.sunvil.co.uk>; and, Tapestry Holidays, tel: 020 8235 7800, <www.tapestryholidays.com>.

Rooms in Private Homes. The cheapest rooms are those that are privately rented. They are almost always clean, and are graded A and B by the local tourist police, though rates are often negotiable.

I'd like a single/double room **Tha íthela éna monóklino/díklino**
with bath/shower **me bánio/dous**
What's the rate per night? **Póso éki/stihízi gia káthe vrádi?**

AIRPORTS

Zákynthos: Located about 5km (3 miles) from Zákynthos Town, this busy airport has been done up and the facilities improved. If you book through a tour operator you will be met at the airport and whisked off to your villa or resort, otherwise you will have to either catch one of the buses on the main Zákynthos Town–Kerí road 1.5km (1 mile) from the airport entrance – these buses are reliable and air-conditioned – or take a taxi into town (around €5). For information on flight arrivals and departures tel: 26950 29500.

Kefalloniá: The airport is near the village of Miniá, about 7km (4 miles) south of Argostóli. The building is modern, with a few basic facilities such as a shop and refreshment stand, but like all island airports it can get very busy during high season. If you are not being met by a tour representative or are picking up a hire car booked in advance, then you have no option but to take a – costly – taxi into town (about €10). For information on arrivals and departures tel: 26710 29900.

B

BICYCLE AND MOTORCYCLE HIRE (RENTAL)

You can hire bicycles and motorcycles in all the tourist centres. However, many package operators warn clients against motorised cycles and scooters for the quite legitimate fear of an accident (and to drum up more business for organised excursions). It is vital that you check that motorbike hire does not invalidate your holiday insurance. Scooter hire is cheap (you should be quoted a rate per day, including third-party insurance and CDW, collision-damage waiver). Terms vary by operator. Usually, to hire a motorbike with an engine larger than 50cc you must be at least 18 years old and hold a full motorcycle licence. It is illegal to ride without a crash helmet, or to drive without an appropriate licence on your person; the spot fines approach €100.

It is certainly not advisable to ride a motorbike in shorts or a swimsuit, since burns or scrapes resulting from even a slight accident could be appalling. Inspect brakes and tyres before hiring, and drive with care. Even on good roads there are occasional potholes.

Bicycle hire is less common, largely because of the mountainous terrain, but on Kefalloniá a good place for serious riders to seek information is the bike shop at the far (non-pedestrianised) end of Lithóstroto.

BUDGETING FOR YOUR TRIP

Greece is certainly not a budget destination these days, and particularly so since the introduction of the euro. However, it is still possible not to spend a fortune on Zákynthos and Kefalloniá, especially if you book an airfare/accommodation package. Otherwise, independent travellers can find decent places to stay for around €50–60 per night for a double room, with discounts available out of the high season.

Eating out is considerably cheaper if you stick to *magirevtá* and simple grills and *mezédes* in places frequented by locals, but generally a three-course meal plus drinks in a decent restaurant or *tavérna* will cost around €15–25 per person. Car hire starts from about €30 per day in low season (including fully comprehensive insurance). Public transport and museum fees are inexpensive.

C

CAMPING

Camping in Greece is permitted only at official sites. There are a couple of sites close to Argostóli on Kefalloniá; on Zákynthos most of the sites are found around Laganás Bay and on the Vasilikós Peninsula. Local tourist offices have lists of campsites.

May we camp here?	**Boroúme na kataskinósoume edó?**
We have a tent	**Éhoume mía skiní**

CAR HIRE (RENTAL)

Unless visiting the islands with the intention of walking or cycling, you might consider hiring a car, especially on Zákynthos, where the bus service is very patchy. As elsewhere in Greece, car hire is not particularly cheap, but it is certainly less expensive than touring by taxi. For a decent family-sized car in high season, you should budget around €300 per week. In summer choose a model with air conditioning.

You'll find car-hire firms throughout the islands, especially in tourist centres. To be on the safe side, reserve a car ahead of time, especially for the high season. Local firms generally charge slightly less than international agencies and provide equally good cars and service. International chains that operate on the islands, bookable through their websites, include Avis, Budget, Europcar, Hertz, National, Sixt and Thrifty.

You will need a credit card for the deposit and a full national licence (held for at least one year) from your country of residence.

Depending on the model and the hire company, the minimum age for hiring a car varies from 21 to 25. Third-party liability insurance (CDW) is usually included in the stated rate, and it is always worth paying a little more for comprehensive coverage.

What's the hire charge for a full day?	**Póso kostízi giá mía méra?**
I'd like to hire a car (tomorrow)	**Tha íthela na nikiáso éna avtokínito (ávrio)**

CLIMATE

July and August are the sunniest, hottest and busiest tourist months. You may prefer to visit between mid-May and late June or from early September to mid-October. At any time outside July (even in August) it might rain. (The Ionians are the greenest of all the Greek island chains.)

In winter it rains very hard. November and December are the wettest months, and January the coldest, but even during these mid-winter doldrums the climate is temperate. Spring, when the islands burst with wild flowers, is the best time for walking.

The chart below shows each month's average air and sea temperature in Celsius and Fahrenheit, and the average number of hours of sunshine per day.

	J	F	M	A	M	J	J	A	S	O	N	D
Air°C	10	10	12	15	19	24	27	26	23	19	15	12
Air°F	50	50	54	59	66	75	81	79	73	66	59	54
Sea°C	15	15	15	16	18	21	24	25	24	21	19	18
Sea°F	59	59	59	61	64	70	75	77	75	70	66	64
Sunshine hours	5	6	7	7	9	10	11	12	9	6	4	3

CLOTHING

Clothing is almost always casual on the islands. However, the Greeks do like to dress up when they go out in the evening, and visitors who make a bit of an effort will be smiled upon (those who turn up in dirty and torn clothing will be regarded as impolite). With regard to comfort, choose lightweight cotton clothing in spring and summer, and a warm jacket, sweater and rainwear in autumn and winter. Since it rains from time to time (outside of July and August), a protective coat or umbrella might be a good idea. Plastic or 'trekking' sandals are extremely useful for stony beaches; these are usually available in some shape or form from beach-side tourist shops, so don't worry if you forget to buy them before you leave home.

CRIME AND SAFETY (see also EMERGENCIES and POLICE)

The Zakynthians and Kefallonians are, like the vast majority of Greek people, scrupulously honest. However, unfortunately, thefts occur more often than they used to on the islands – usually ascribed to migrant Albanian and Romanian workers, but more often it turns out to be fellow holidaymakers – so it's sensible to leave valuables in the hotel safe. Take care of your passport, but at the same time be aware that you're required to have official ID on your person at all times in Greece.

Possession of drugs is a very serious matter in Greece, carrying a stiff mandatory sentence. Make sure you have a prescription from your doctor if you will be carrying syringes, insulin, any narcotic drugs or even codeine, which is illegal in Greece.

CUSTOMS AND ENTRY REQUIREMENTS

All EU citizens can enter Greece to visit or work for an unlimited length of time. British citizens must be in possession of a valid passport. Citizens of Ireland can enter with a valid identity card or passport.

Citizens of the US, Canada, Australia and New Zealand can stay for up to three months on production of a valid passport. South African citizens can stay for up to two months on production of a valid passport. No visas are needed for these stays. If you wish to extend these timescales you must obtain a permit from the proper department of either Zákynthos Town or Argostóli police stations.

Greece has strict regulations about importing drugs. All the obvious ones are illegal, and there are strong punitive measures for anyone breaking the rules. Codeine and some tranquillisers are also banned. If you take any drug on the advice of your doctor, carry enough for your needs in an official container, as medicines for personal use are permitted.

Since the abolition of duty-free allowances for all EU countries, all goods brought into Greece from Britain and Ireland must be duty-paid. In theory there are no limitations to the amount of duty-paid goods that can be brought into the country. However, cigarettes and most spirits are much cheaper in Greece than in Britain and Ireland (government duty is much lower, so waiting until you reach your destination to buy these goods will save you money).

For citizens of non-EU countries, allowances for duty-free goods brought into Greece are: 200 cigarettes or 50 cigars or 250g of tobacco; 1 litre of spirits or 4 litres of wine; 250ml of cologne or 50ml of perfume.

Non-EU residents can claim back Value Added Tax (currently between 6 and 18 percent) on any items costing over €120, provided they export the item within 90 days of purchase. Tax-rebate forms are available at tourist shops and department stores. Keep the receipt and form. Make your claim at the customs area of the airport when departing.

Currency Restrictions. There are no limits on the amount of euros visitors can import or export. There are no restrictions on travellers cheques, but cash sums of more than $10,000 or its equivalent should be declared on entry.

D

DRIVING

Road Conditions. The surfaces on main roads are generally very good, though curves in the road are often indicated too late, are sometimes unsignposted and are never banked. If there is a mirror on a bend, slow down to a low gear, it is probably going to be extremely tight or narrow, or perhaps both.

On many clifftop roads it is very dangerous to pass, so be patient if there is a slow-moving bus or heavy vehicle in front of you. Conversely, try to let local speed maniacs pass you as soon as it is safe to do so.

The secondary roads are some of the narrowest on any of the Greek islands – it's difficult to safely exceed 50kph (31mph) – while anything marked 'unsurfaced' on a map can be very rough indeed. Rockslides are common in the rainy season, and broken shoulders or potholes are not unknown on even the best-paved stretches. Drive with extreme caution, as you might be responsible for damage sustained to the underside of your hire car, even with comprehensive coverage.

NB Zákynthos has a reputation for having some of the most dangerous roads in Greece, be very careful.

Driving Regulations. Drive on the right side and pass on the left. Traffic from the right has right of way. A Greek practice to be aware of is that if a driver flashes the lights, it means 'Stay

Are we on the right road for…?	**Eímaste sto sostó drómo gia…?**
Fill the tank please, with (unleaded) petrol	**Parakaló, geméste i dexamení me amólivdi**
My car has broken down	**To avtokínito mou éhi ragisméni**
There's been an accident	**Eínai distíhimai**

where you are, I'm coming through', not 'Go ahead'. Seat belts are obligatory, as is the carrying of your driving licence while at the wheel; there is an €86 spot fine if you are caught without it. The speed limit is 80kph (50mph) inside built-up areas, 100kph (62mph) outside. In practice, however, the winding roads usually set the speed limit.

Fuel. Generally you will never be far from a filling station, though in parts of the north and west of Zákynthos, and the north and centre of Kefalloniá, they are fairly few and far between. Note that in rural areas filling stations are open only until about 7pm and closed on Sunday. On busy main roads and in resorts they open daily from early until late.

If You Need Help. For breakdown and accident assistance phone the Greek motoring club (ELPA), tel. 104, which has a reciprocal arrangement with most other national motoring associations. Some car-hire companies have agreements with other roadside emergency companies, such as Hellas Service (tel: 157).

Road Signs. On main roads and at junctions these will be in Greek and Latin (Western) letters; on secondary roads they may just be in Greek (for some important ones see the list below).

Detour	Παράκαψη/**Parákapsi**
Parking	Πάρκιγκ/**Párking**
No parking	...απαγορέυεται/...**apagorévetai**
Be careful	Προσοχή/**Prosohí**
Bus stop	Στάση λεοφορίο/**Stasí leoforío**
Stop	Σταμάτα/**Stamáta**
Pedestrians	Για πεζούς/**Gia pezoús**
Danger	Κίνδινος, επικίνδινος/**Kíndinos, epikíndinos**
No entry	Απαγορέυεται η είσοδος/**Apagorévetai i eísodos**

E

ELECTRICITY

Greece has 220-volt/50-cycle AC current. Sockets are two-pin, so bring an adapter or transformer with you as necessary.

a transformer	**énas metashimatistís**
an adapter	**énas prosarmostís**

EMBASSIES AND CONSULATES *(presvía; proxenío)*

There is a United Kingdom consular office in Zákynthos Town. Embassies of all major countries are located in Athens. From outside Greece, dial the country code 30 before the 10-digit number.

British Consulate: Fóskolou 5, Zákynthos Town; tel: 26950 22906/48030; fax: 26950 23769.

Embassies in Athens:

Australia: D. Soútsou 37; tel: 21064 50404.

Canada: Gennadíou 4; tel: 21072 73400.

Ireland: Vassiléos Konstantínou 7 ; tel: 21072 32771.

New Zealand: Xenía 24; tel: 21077 10112.

South Africa: Leofóros Kifissías 60; tel: 21068 06645.

UK: Ploutárhou 1; tel: 21072 36211.

US: Vassilísis Sofías 91; tel: 21072 12951.

EMERGENCIES

Police: (all-purpose emergency number) **100**; (Zákynthos Town) 26950 83083; (Argostóli) 26710 22200.

Tourist Police: **171**; (Zákynthos Town) 26950 24450; (Argostóli) 26710 22815.

Hospitals: (Zákynthos Town) 26950 59100/59168; (Argostóli) 26710 24641/23230.

Ambulance: **166**; (Zákynthos Town) 26950 23166.

Fire: 199.
Vehicle emergency: 104 or **157**.
Port Authority: (Zákynthos Town) 26950 28117; (Argostóli)
26710 22224.

Fire!	**Fotiá!**
Help!	**Voíthia!**
Police!	**Astynomía!**
Stop!	**Stamatíste!**

G

GETTING THERE

It is possible to cross Europe overland and take the ferry from Italy to
Pátra on the Greek mainland, and then a ferry to either Sámi on Kefalloniá, or, from Kyllíni, further down the coast, to Zákynthos Town.
From the UK it is probably better to fly into Athens (the low-cost
airlines easyJet <www.easyjet.com> and Hellas Jet <www.hellas-
jet.com> both fly to Athens from London) and then either connect for
the Olympic (<www.olympic-airways.gr>) internal flights to the
islands (45 minutes), or take the coach from the Kifissoú bus station
(several daily to Zákynthos and Argostóli, around 7 hours; all coaches
connect with ferries for which there is a small additional cost).

During the summer, another way to reach the islands is by charter
flight. Flights from the UK, which link several British airports to
Zákynthos and Kefalloniá, take around 3 hours.

H

HEALTH AND MEDICAL CARE

In theory, EU citizens with an E111 form (obtainable in their own
country) can get free treatment under the Greek health service.

However, you are likely to receive the minimum treatment and must pay for medication, and state hospital facilities are over-stretched in the tourist season. It's therefore essential to obtain private medical insurance for your holiday. Doctors and dentists are concentrated in Zákynthos Town and Argostóli; your hotel or apartment owner will be able to find you one who speaks English. Most resorts have a local medical clinic.

Hospitals. The hospitals in Zákynthos Town and Argostóli operate a 24-hour emergency service (tel: 166, or, Zákynthos: tel: 26950 59100/59168; Argostóli tel: 26710 24641/23230). Otherwise call the tourist police (Zákynthos tel: 26950 27367; Argostóli tel: 26710 22815).

Pharmacies (ΦΑΡΜΑΚΕΙΟ – *farmakío* in singular). A red or green cross on a white background identifies a chemist (pharmacy). They are normally open only during the morning Monday to Friday, but a notice on the door should tell you the nearest one for after-hours service. One pharmacy is always open in Zákynthos Town and Argostóli at night and on Saturday and Sunday. Without a prescription, you can't get sleeping pills, barbiturates, or medicine for stomach upsets.

Mosquitoes (non-malarial) can be a nuisance on the islands, so bring along mosquito repellent. Sunburn is a very real danger in the hot Mediterranean sun; cover up or use a high-factor sunscreen. While swimming look out for sea urchins – their black spines are very sharp and will break off in your skin. If this happens, seek medical attention, as they are very tricky to remove.

a doctor/dentist	**énas giatrós/odontogiatrós**
hospital	**nosokomío**
an upset stomach	**varystomahiá**
sunstroke	**ilíasi**
a fever	**pyretós**

HOLIDAYS

Banks, offices and shops are closed on the following national holidays, as well as during some feasts and festivals (*see also the Calendar of Events on page 93*):

1 January	*Protokroniá*	New Year's Day
6 January	*Ágia Theofánia*	Epiphany
25 March	*Ikostipébti Martíou (tou Evangelismoú)*	Greek Independence Day
1 May	*Protomagiá*	May Day
15 August	*Dekapendávgoustos (tis Panagías)*	Assumption Day
28 October	*Ikostiogdóïs Oktovríou*	*Óhi* ('No') Day, celebrating defiance of the 1940 Italian ultimatum
25 December	*Hristoúgenna*	Christmas Day
26 December	*Sýnaxi Theotókou*	Meeting of Virgin's Entourage

Moveable dates:

Katharí Deftéra	1st day of Lent: 'Clean Monday'
Megáli Paraskeví	Good Friday
Pásha	Easter
tou Agíou Pnévmatos	Whit (Pentecost) Sunday and Monday ('Holy Spirit'), June

Note: These moveable holidays are celebrated according to dates in the Greek Orthodox calendar, which often differ from Catholic or Protestant dates.

L

LANGUAGE

Only in remote countryside spots will non-Greek-speaking tourists run into serious communication problems. You will find that basic

English is spoken almost everywhere. Stress is a very important feature of the Greek language, denoted by an accent above the vowel of the syllable to be emphasised. The table above lists the Greek letters in their upper- and lower-case forms, followed by the closest individual or combined letters to which they correspond in English.

A	α	a	as in *father*
B	β	v	as in *veto*
Γ	γ	g	as in *go* (except before *i* and *e* sounds, when it's like the *y* in *yes*)
Δ	δ	d	sounds like **th** in *this*
E	ε	e	as in *get*
Z	ζ	z	as in English
H	η	i	as in *ski*
Θ	θ	th	as in *thin*
I	ι	i	as in *ski*
K	κ	k	as in English
Λ	λ	l	as in English
M	μ	m	as in English
N	ν	n	as in English
Ξ	ξ	x	as in *box*
O	ο	o	as in *top*
Π	π	p	as in English
P	ρ	r	as in English
Σ	σ	s	as in *kiss*, except like *z* before *m* or *g* sounds
T	τ	t	as in English
Y	υ	y	as in *country*
Φ	φ	f	as in English
X	χ	h	as in Scottish *loch*
Ψ	ψ	ps	as in *tipsy*
Ω	ω	o	as in *long*

M

MAPS

The best maps available of Zákynthos and Argostóli are by Road Editions. They are clear and accurate and give place names in both Greek letters and in transliteration. Available across the islands, you can also obtain them from Stanfords in the UK (tel: 020 7836 1321).

MEDIA

Bookshops. English-language books of the airport-lounge type can be found in shops in all the resorts, anything more highbrow is harder to come by.

Internet Cafés. Internet access is now available in almost every beach resort. Charges are typically €2 to €4 per hour.

Newspapers and Magazines *(evimerídes; periodiká)*. During the tourist season, foreign-language newspapers are on sale at shops and kiosks on the island, generally on the day after publication. The only Greek English-language paper is the *Athens News* (€1.50, every Friday).

Television *(tiliérasi)*. Most hotels and many bars offer satellite television networks, including CNN, BBC World and Sky.

Radio. BBC World Service is broadcast on the short-wave band (try 15.07mhz and 12.09mhz), but reception is poor.

MONEY

Currency *(nómisma)*. In common with most other Western European countries, the euro (EUR or €) is the official currency used in Greece. Notes are in denominations of 5, 10, 20, 50, 100 and 500 euros; coins are 1 and 2 euros and 1, 2, 5, 10, 20 and 50 cents.

Banks and Currency Exchange: You'll find banks in Zákynthos Town, Argostóli and in the larger resort areas. Hotels and travel agencies (the latter sometimes called 'tourist offices') are authorised to change money, but you will probably get less for your money than you would from a bank. You'll need your passport as identification to change travellers cheques (but not to change cash).

ATMs. The easiest method to obtain cash is through 'hole-in-the-wall' cash dispensers. These can be found in Zákynthos Town, Argostóli and in all of the larger resorts (though not Fiskárdo). Depending upon your own individual card fees, this might also be the cheapest way to get money.

Credit Cards *(pistotikés kártes)*. The major credit cards are accepted in many shops and by car-hire firms, most hotels, more expensive restaurants and some (but not all) filling stations. Be aware that you might have to pay an additional 5 to 7 percent for the privilege of using plastic. They are also not very cost-effective for use in ATMs, attracting fees of about 4 to 5 percent. It is also possible, for a fee, to obtain cash on a credit card at some banks.

Travellers Cheques. Most major brands of travellers cheques – in any Western currency – are readily cashed. Always take your passport for identification.

I want to change some pounds/dollars travellers cheques	**Thélo na alláxo merikés líres/meriká dollária taxidiotikés epitagés**
Can I pay with this credit card?	**Boró na pliróso me avtí tin pistotikí kárta?**

OPENING HOURS

The siesta (the traditional Mediterranean early afternoon break) is still alive and well on Zákynthos and Kefalloniá, and observed most strictly outside tourist areas.

Shops. Traditional hours are generally Mon–Sat 8.30 or 9am–2 or 2.30pm. On Tuesday, Thursday and Friday shops reopen in the evening from 5.30 or 6pm until 8.30–9pm. Shops catering to tourists often stay open through the siesta and until late each evening in the summer, as well as part of Sunday. Larger supermarkets open Mon–Fri 8.30am–8.30pm and Sat 9am–6pm.

Museums and Tourist Attractions. Hours vary greatly, but it is worth noting that state-run museums are closed on Monday. Museums are typically open Tues–Sat 8.30am–3pm and Sun 8.30 or 9.30am–2.30 or 3pm.

Banks. Mon–Thur 8am–2.30pm and Fri 8.30am–2pm.

Post Offices. Mon–Fri 7.30am–2pm.

Businesses and Offices. 8am–1pm, then 2pm–5pm. Government offices work 8am–1.30pm, sometimes 2.30pm, and don't reopen.

Restaurants and *Tavérnes*. More traditional establishments open for lunch from noon until around 3.30pm and for dinner from 7pm to around 11.30pm. More tourist-oriented establishments might open early for breakfast or coffee and stay open throughout the day.

P

POLICE

Emergency telephone number: **100**.
Tourist police: Zákynthos, tel: 26950 27367; Argostóli, tel: 26710 22815.

The tourist police (*touristikí astynomía*) have a specific mission to help visitors to the island, as well as to accompany state inspectors of hotels and restaurants to ensure that proper standards and prices are maintained.

If you need to report a loss or theft to the police, go to the police station closest to the scene of the crime. Each group of villages has a police station; you'll have to enquire locally for its location.

Traffic police check car documents and driving licences, operate speed traps and issue fines for illegal parking (fines in Greece are high). Car-hire companies will use your credit-card details to pay ignored parking tickets; you have 10 working days to pay moving violations in person. Failing that, a court date will be set, and a summons sent to your home address. Failure to appear will result in an extra conviction for contempt of court, and make future re-entry to Greece extremely difficult.

Where's the nearest police station?	**Pou íne to kondinótero astynomikó tmíma?**

POST OFFICES

Post offices (ELTA) handle letters, parcels and money orders, but no longer exchange foreign currency. Look for a blue sign with the head of Hermes traced on it in yellow.

Post offices are generally open Mon–Fri 7.30am–2pm. Registered letters and parcels to non-EU destinations are checked before being sent, so don't seal them until presenting them at the desk. The main post office in Zákynthos Town is on Tertséti (open Mon–Fri 8am–10pm), in Argostóli it is found on Lithóstroto (open as above).

Stamps are also sold at the majority of shops and hotels selling postcards. The price for sending a postcard to all overseas countries is €0.60. Delivery to Europe takes from 4 to 10 days.

Letterboxes are yellow, but make sure you use the one marked *exoterikó* (abroad). In tourist hotels, the receptionist will take care of dispatching your mail.

Have you received any mail for…?	**éhete grámmata giá…?**
A stamp for this letter/ postcard	**Éna grammatósimo giavtó to grámma/giavtí tin kart postál**
express (special delivery)	**katepígon**
registered	**systiméno**

PUBLIC TRANSPORT

Buses *(leofória)*. The public bus service on Zákynthos is patchy, but, where it does exist, it is very good value. Timetables are displayed at bus stops (**ΣΤΑΣΙΣ** – *stásis*) and at the KTEL bus station on Filitá in Zákynthos Town (tel: 26950 22255/42656). Most services run between Zákynthos Town and Laganás Bay and Vasilikós. For all buses, buy your tickets on board or from nearby kiosks. You can flag a bus down anywhere within reason; it will also drop you off between stops, if possible.

The service on Kefalloniá is much better, making touring the island by public transport a real possibility. Direct buses run between Argostóli (on A. Trítsi, tel: 26710 22276) and all the other major towns (Póros, Sámi, Agía Evfimía and Fiskárdo), and between Fiskárdo, Sámi, Póros and Skála. The Pallikí Peninsula is less well served, but there is service between Lixoúri and Xí. There is also a regular local service between Argostóli and Lássi. The fares are very reasonable and, generally, the service is frequent and punctual.

Taxis. These are an expensive way to get around, but may be your only option in parts of Zákynthos. Make sure the meter is switched on; there are two rates depending on time of day and whether you are inside or outside town. Radio taxis can be summoned, for which there's a small surcharge.

Ferries. Regular ferries run between Pátra on the mainland and Sámi on Kefalloniá, and Kyllíni and Zákynthos Town. There is also a ferry from Ágios Nikólaos, in the north of Zákynthos, to the tiny port of Pesáda on Kefalloniá. A ferry runs between Sámi and Píso Aetós on Itháki. For current ferry schedules and fares check with your nearest travel agent or the port authority *(see page 113)*.

What's the fare to…?	**Póso éhi éna isitírio giá…?**
When's the next bus to…?	**Póte févgi to epómeno leoforío giá…?**

R

RELIGION

The national religion of Greece is Greek Orthodox. You must dress modestly to visit churches and monasteries, which normally means long trousers for men, a long skirt or trousers for women and covered shoulders for both sexes. However, men might be allowed to wear long shorts, and skirts may be provided at the back of churches for women to wrap around themselves.

T

TELEPHONES

Local Calling. There are no longer any area codes as such in Greece; even within the same local-call zone you must dial all 10 digits of the number. What were the old codes are now merely the locators: 26950 for all of Zákynthos; 26710 for Argostóli, Lixoúri and the southwest; and 26740 for the east coast and north from Póros to Fiskárdo, and the island of Itháki.

From Overseas. To call Greece from abroad, first dial the international access code (00 from the UK), then **30** (the country code for Greece) and finally all 10 digits of the local number.

Long Distance from Greece. International direct dialling is available at street-corner phone booths. These take phonecards, which are the cheapest (if least private and noisiest) way to phone home. To reverse charges (collect calls), dial 151 for Europe and 161 for the rest of the world. In higher-grade hotels you can dial long-distance from your room, but charges can be exorbitant – much more than using a mobile. All UK mobile providers have roaming agreements with at least one of the four Greek companies. NOAH American users must have a tri-band mobile to get a signal in Greece. Overseas directory assistance is through the international operator (dial 161). For the local operator, dial 132.

Coin Phones. These are not particularly common and tend to be countertop models in cafés and kiosks. They take small denomination euro coins.

Fax Service. Fax services are available at major hotels, post offices and some travel agencies.

reverse-charge (collect) call	**plirotéo apó to paralípti**

TIME DIFFERENCES

Greek time is GMT plus two hours. Daylight saving, when Greek clocks are put forward one hour, is observed from the last Sunday of March to the last Sunday of October. The chart shows the times in Greece and various other places during the European summer.

New York	London	Paris	**Greece**	Sydney	Auckland
5am	10am	11am	**noon**	8pm	9pm

TIPPING

The Greeks aren't obsessed with tipping, but it is the norm to leave a little more if service has been good. The list below gives the usual amounts to leave:

Hotel porter	up to €2
Hotel maid	€1 per day
Waiter	5–10 percent
Taxi driver	10 percent
Hairdresser/barber	10 percent
Lavatory attendant	€0.30

TOILETS

Public conveniences are best avoided. A better option is to use facilities at museums or the better cafés. If you do drop in specifically to use the toilet, it's customary to purchase coffee or some other drink before leaving.

Important note: you are always expected to put toilet tissue in the waste bin rather than down the toilet. Due to their narrow-bore pipes, toilets easily become clogged.

Where are the toilets?	**Pou íne i toualéttes?**

TOURIST INFORMATION

The Greek National Tourist Organization (*Ellinikós Organismós Tourismoú*, abbreviated EOT) has the following offices abroad:

Australia: 51–7 Pitt Street, Sydney, NSW 2000; tel: (02) 9241 1663.
Canada: 91 Scollard Street, 2nd Floor, Toronto, Ontario M5R 1GR; tel: (416) 968 2220.
UK: 4 Conduit Street, London W1R 0DJ; tel: 020 7734 5997.
US: 645 Fifth Avenue, New York, NY 10022; tel: (212) 421 5777.

These offices supply general information and glossy pictures, but when it comes to anything specific on Zákynthos or Kefalloniá they are usually of little help.

Zákynthos, strangely, does not have an official (EOT) tourism office, but you could try asking the tourist police for information. The Kefalloniá office in Argostóli (open daily 8am–2.30pm; on A. Trítsi, near the port authority; tel: 26710 22248) breaks the mould by being both helpful and informative.

It is much easier to get local information from a travel agency (some of these actually call themselves 'tourist offices'). But you should remember that their information might not be impartial, as they have a vested interest in selling you excursions or at least in pointing you in certain directions. However, one recommended agency is Pama Travel in Fiskárdo, Kefalloniá (tel: 26740 41033).

W

WATER

Tap water is safe to drink all over Zákynthos and Kefalloniá: in some places it may even come from a nearby spring. People with sensitive stomachs should be a little careful at first, as the water is extremely hard. However, drinking tap and spring water is much more environmentally friendly than drinking 'mineral' water from the ubiquitous plastic bottles; visitors should take their own water bottle and refill it as often as possible.

WEBSITES

There are now a number of useful websites for people travelling to Zákynthos and Kefalloniá:

- <www.gnto.gr> (the official site of the EOT)
- <www.culture.gr> (the site of the Ministry of Culture, giving useful information on museums and archaeological sites)
- <www.ferries.gr> (an excellent site giving online timetables for most Greek ferry routes)
- <www.ktel.org> (the national bus network)
- <www.zakynthos.gr> (the official site of the prefecture)
- <www.kefalonia.gr> (the same, in Greek only but with useful links to other – English-language – sites)
- <www.foi.org.uk> (the very useful site of Friends of the Ionian, an organisation that seeks to promote the islands' culture and identity, while protecting their environment)
- <www.archelon.gr> (Sea Turtle Protection Society of Greece)
- <www.earthseasky.org> (site of a conservation organisation based on Zákynthos)
- <www.nmp-zak.org> (the National Marine Park of Zákynthos)

WEIGHTS AND MEASURES

Like most of Europe, Greece uses the metric system.

Recommended Hotels

Many hotels get booked up quickly for the high season (from mid-June until October and, in particular, around the middle of August), so make sure that you reserve well ahead. To telephone a hotel, dial the international country code for Greece (30), followed by the 10-digit number provided in our listings.

All hotels are classified by the Greek National Tourist Organization: luxury (L) class is at the very top, then A class down to E class (only hotels of L, A, B and C classes are featured below). In 2003, a star system (five-star equal to L, four-star to A, etc) was introduced, but has been slow to catch on. Rating establishes minimum price rates, but prices can often vary widely within each class according to the season, location and availability of rooms. By law, rates must always be posted in all rooms; in practice this is often ignored.

The price categories below are for a double room with bath per night in high season. All hotel room rates include VAT (Value Added Tax) of 18 percent. All L- and A-class hotels have air conditioning. Many hotels in beach resorts are open only from April to October. Those in Zákynthos Town and Argostóli are open all year round.

€€€€   above 130 euros
€€€   90–130 euros
€€   60–90 euros
€   below 60 euros

ZÁKYNTHOS

ZÁKYNTHOS TOWN

Hotel Alba €€ *Lábrou Zivá 38, Zákynthos Town; tel: 26950 26641.* This small, newish B-class hotel is located in a fairly quiet area just two blocks in from the seafront. Facilities include air conditioning, television in the rooms and room service.

Hotel Bitzaro €€ *Dionysíou Róma, Zákynthos Town; tel: 26950 23644*. This is a decent option, located near to the town beach. The building is ivy-covered, and the quiet rooms have a television and ceiling fans.

Hotel Palatino €€€€ *Kolokotróni 10 and Kolivá, Zákynthos Town; tel: 26950 27780, fax: 26950 45400;* <www.palatinohotel.gr>. Zákynthos Town's most upmarket option, refurbished in 1999 and professionally run. The rooms, designed for business travellers, have all the trimmings, and the hotel as a whole has been well cared for. A buffet breakfast is provided, and there is also a restaurant.

Hotel Strada Marina €€€ *Lobárdou 14, Zákynthos Town; tel: 26950 42761–3, fax: 26950 28733;* <*e-mail:* stradamarina@aias.gr>. The largest place in Zákynthos Town, with comfortable but not overly exciting rooms. It's a prominent, modern building close to Platía Solomoú, and some of the rooms have great views of the harbour. Breakfast is included, and there is a rooftop pool.

VASILIKÓS AND LAGANÁS BAY

Levantino Studio Apartments €€ *9km (5½ miles) from Vasilikós; tel: 26950 35366, fax: 26950 35173;* <www.levantino-apps.gr>. Ten quiet and attractive apartments close to the sea at the far end of the Vasilikos Peninsula. All are equipped with a kitchen, and some look out over the gardens and sea. Discounts available out of high season.

Liuba's Holiday Houses €€ *800m (875yds) before Yérakas beach car-park; tel: 26950 35372, 26950 35313 or 69761 35319*. High-standard, tile-roofed and wood-trimmed bungalows that sleep two to four. They are picturesquely scattered across a field and hillside. Apr–Oct.

Hotel Matilda €€€ *Vasilikós district; tel: 26950 35376;* <www.matildahotel.gr>. A designer, B-class hotel on a hilltop, with commanding sea views from all its rooms and a large pool terrace. The hotel was renovated in 2001.

Porto Koukla Beach Hotel €€€ *Lithakiá; tel: 26950 52393/ 51577, fax: 26950 52391/52392;* <www.pavlos.gr>. A large hotel at the western end of Laganás Bay. Popular with German and Austrian visitors, it is well away from the tawdriness further east. The gardens back on to a narrow beach, which is overlooked by the hotel's excellent, and cheap, *tavérna*.

Sirocco Hotel €€ *Kalamáki; tel: 26950 26083–6, fax: 26950 26087;* <www.siroccohotel.gr>. This is a good and reasonably quiet option for Kalamaki; the renovated and stylish standard rooms are a bargain out of season. There is a large pool set in an attractive garden, and the beach is not too far away.

Villa Katerina €€ *Porto Roma, Vasilikós; tel: 26950 35456;* <www.villakaterina.com>. These two buildings, in pretty gardens, have simple rooms with kitchenettes and attached bathrooms. Set back from the beach the rooms are very quiet, and the surrounding area is lovely.

Villa Petunia €€€€ *Lithakiá. Contact: Betty Andronikos, tel: 69322 60534;* <*e-mail:* androel@hol.gr>. This huge, beautifully furnished villa is set on a hill above the village. Surrounded by flowers, with a fabulous view over Laganás Bay and the mountains, the villa sleeps 10 to 12 people and has every conceivable appliance, from DVD player to espresso machine. There is a new swimming pool, and organic eggs, oil and vegetables are available from the garden.

THE NORTH

Comtessa Estate €€ *Akrotíri. Book through: Sunisle; tel: (00 44) 0871 222 1226;* <www.sunisle.co.uk>. A tranquil, stone-built aristocratic estate full of character and set in gorgeous surroundings. Accommodation is in either the large manor house, full of heirlooms of the Komoutou family, or the smaller but equally lovely Garden Cottage. Steps down to the sea lead to a private bathing platform. The Comtessa Maria is a charming host, and the spectacular views and sense of history all add to the experience.

Iberostar Plagos Beach €€€ *Aboúla Beach, Tsiliví; tel: 26950 62800, fax: 26950 62900;* <www.iberostar.com>. Previously the Louis Plagos Beach, this is a large resort hotel with a huge range of facilities, particularly for children. The rooms are plain but large and have balconies, and there is the inevitable, but good, hotel pool and restaurant.

Ionian Star Hotel €€ *Alykés; tel: 26950 83416/83658, fax: 26950 83173;* <www.ionian-star.gr>. A smallish and very well kept hotel. The spotless rooms are excellent value (breakfast is included) and there is a restaurant which specialises in Greek food.

Montreal Hotel €€ *Alykés; tel: 26950 83241/83341, fax: 26950 83342;* <www.montreal.gr>. The Montreal Hotel is a modern hotel block, but it's attractive enough and covered in flowers. It has its own pool and beach club. The plain, clean and well-maintained rooms have balconies looking over the sea. There is also an average restaurant, which dishes up an eclectic mix of food, from pizza to Greek salad.

Nobelos Apartments €€€€ *Ágios Nikólaos; tel: 26950 27632/ 31400, fax: 26950 31131/29277;* <*e-mail:* nobelos@otenet.gr>. These luxury apartments in the north of the island are hideously expensive but lovely. The four tastefully decorated suites are in a traditional stone-built house, each with an individual character. Along with excellent service, breakfast is provided and there's a secluded bay for swimming close by.

Hotel Tsamis Camelot €€€ *Paralía Kypséli; tel: 26950 62962;* <*e-mail:* htsamis@otenet.gr>. A-class bungalows and a hotel-wing complex, built on a human scale. They have large rooms and access to a pool right on the shoreline.

The Windmill € *Korithí, Cape Skinári; tel: 26950 31132*. One of the most attractive places to stay on Zákynthos. It consists of one room in a converted windmill at the very north end of the island, close to the Blue Caves. If you really want to get away from it all, this might well be your best option.

Zante Palace €€ *Tsiliví; tel: 26950 490490, fax: 26950 49092;* <www.zantepalace.com>. This huge, newly built, hotel is on the bluff overlooking Tsiliví Bay, giving great views across to Kefalloniá. For what's on offer the rooms (which look out over the bay) are good value, and there is a nicely sited pool.

KEFALLONIA

ARGOSTÓLI

Aenos Hotel €€€ *Platía Vallianoú, Argostóli; tel: 26710 28013, fax: 26710 27035;* <www.aenos.com>. This, and the Hotel Ionian Plaza (below), are the two best places to stay on the town's central square. The uncluttered pastel-shaded rooms with large attached bathrooms probably give the Aenos the edge; it is also marginally quieter.

Hotel Ionian Plaza €€ *Platía Vallianoú, Argostóli; tel: 26710 25581–4, fax: 26710 25585.* Excellent-value, C-class, designer hotel, with modern bathrooms and balconies overlooking the palm-studded square. The rooms are on the small side, but the staff are friendly. Open all year.

Le Mirage Apartments €€ *Ioan. Tsigante, Argostóli; tel: 26710 24312, fax: 26710 22339;* <www.lemirage.gr>. Simple, but very clean and comfortable, three-room apartments, with fairly limited cooking facilities. Each living room has a balcony, and those facing east have a wonderful view over the bay and Mount Énos (compensation for the steep climb up from town); rooms on the west overlook the well-watered garden.

LIXOÚRI AND THE SOUTH

Belvedere Apartments €€ *Póros; tel: 26740 72493–4, fax: 26740 72083.* A small complex of apartments in the centre of town. Although fairly simple – the standard package of small kitchenette, bedroom and bathroom – they are not without charm, and all have balconies looking over the sea.

Caretta's Nest €€€ *Kamínia Beach, near Skála. Book through: Simply Ionian; tel: (00 44) 020 8541 2202; <www.simplytravel.co. uk>.* A cluster of modern, well-furnished apartments by the deserted Kamínia beach. A great place to get away from it all, but to get into Skála or Kateliós to eat you will need transport or be prepared to walk.

Kastro Hotel €€ *Sámi; tel: 26740 22656/22282, fax: 26740 23004; <e-mail: kastrohotel@hotmail.com>.* A little way out of town, but close to the sea, this is a medium-sized, good-value B-class hotel. The good, if smallish, rooms either look out over the pool and sea or the mountains. Breakfast is provided, and there is also a restaurant.

Lara €€ *Loudáta (Paralía Lourdás); tel: 26710 31157; <e-mail: larab@hol.gr>.* A peaceful, family-run C-class hotel, set in an olive grove some 300m (330yds) above the long beach.

Odysseus Palace €€–€€€ *Póros; tel: 26740 72036, fax: 26740 72148; <www.odysseuspalace.com>.* This modern, newish hotel is the most comfortable place to stay in town. Good discounts may be available for the large and airy rooms (studios and apartments). Being away from the seafront, the hotel is quieter than most. Open all year.

Panas Hotel €€–€€€ *Platía Spartiá; tel: 26710 69506/69448, fax: 26710 69505; <www.panas-kefalonia.com>.* A largish but pleasant B-class hotel on Lourdáta Bay, close to a good beach. The rooms, all of which have a balcony, are fine, if a little unimaginative. The hotel does, however, have good facilities for children, including their own pool and play area. There are also a couple of restuarants and a poolside bar.

Poseidon €€ *Lixoúri; tel: 26710 92518, fax: 26710 91374.* A smallish C-class hotel that gets some package tours. There is no pool, but the gardens lead right down to a beach.

Hotel Summery €€ *Lixoúri; tel: 26710 91771/91871, fax: 26710 91062; <www.hotelsummery.gr>.* A large but quiet hotel on Lixoúri's beach (to the south of town) that mainly caters to tour groups. The rooms are clean and unfussy, and some have balconies. For the amenities on offer (pool, plenty of sporty activities, and a shop) the prices are quite reasonable.

Tara Beach €€–€€€ *Skála; tel: 26710 83341, fax: 26710 83344; <www.tarabeach.gr>.* A large but unobstrusive hotel right on the excellent beach. The rooms are decent, and, if you can't be bothered to waddle the few metres to the sea, there is a good pool in the pleasant gardens, beside which is a handy bar.

White Rocks Hotel and Bungalows €€€ *Platýs Yialós, Argostóli; tel: 26710 28332–5, fax: 26710 28755; <e-mail: whiterocks@otenet.gr>.* Large, A-class resort hotel and bungalow complex behind the closest really good beach to Argostóli. A well-kept and updated 1970s pile, with a certain period charm. Willing staff and good restaurants complete the picture.

THE NORTH

Agnantia Apartments €€€ *Tselendáta, Fiskárdo; tel: 26740 51802–3, fax: 26740 51801; <www.agnantia.com>.* Very well maintained and beautifully located (although a little way out of Fiskárdo), these new rooms stacked up on a hillside are a lovely place to stay. As well as friendly and efficient service, the rooms are tasteful and comfortable, with a small kitchen area, and most have a balcony with wonderful views over to Itháki. A good, and generous, breakfast is included.

The Architect's House €€€ *Ásos. Book through: Simply Ionian; tel: (00 44) 020 8541 2202; <www.simplytravel.co.uk>.* This lovely traditional building, one of the few places to stay in Ásos itself, has three double bedrooms and is down by the harbour. There is plenty of space – a separate living room and kitchen – and the beach and good places to eat are close by.

Emelisse Art Hotel €€€€ *Éblissi, near Fiskárdo; tel: 26106 24900; <www.hospitality.gr>.* Expensive (A-class) but chic, this boutique hotel is set in a traditional building. The well-designed rooms have luxurious bathrooms, and, inevitably, the infinity pool has a lovely view. For this sort of money you should expect to be pampered, and the service lives up to expectations.

Ennea Mouses €€€ *Skála; tel: 26710 83563, fax: 26710 83560.* This is an attractively designed bungalow complex set in well-tended gardens just above mid-beach, with the room interiors doing justice to the surroundings. Officially C-class but priced (and equipped) as B.

Erissos €€€ *Fiskárdo; tel: 26740 41319.* One of the best and most attractive hotels in town. It consists of a few comfortable, upstairs rooms in an old house a few steps back from the quay, next to the Alpha Bank.

Filoxenia €€€ *Fiskárdo; tel: 26740 41319.* A traditionally furnished 19th-century house, beautifully renovated as a small hotel. In the centre of the village, right next to the water.

Moustakis Hotel €€ *Agía Evfimía; tel: 26740 61060/61030, mobile: 693 419 7495; <e-mail:* moustakishotel@hotmail.com>. Smallish, and tucked away behind the harbourfront, this is the most pleasant hotel in town. All the rooms have air conditioning and balconies. Breakfast is available (extra charge). Discounts available for long stays.

The Olive Grove €€€ *Evreti. Book through: Sunvil; tel: (00 44) 020 8568 4499; <www.sunvil.co.uk>.* This stone-built traditional house (dates from 1836) about 6km (4 miles) south of Fiskárdo is in a wonderful position surrounded by fir trees and looking out to Itháki. Although kitted out with a modern kitchen and bathrooms, it still retains its local feel. As well as a nearby secluded pebble beach (with the clearest water), there is a lovely pool.

Panormos €€ *Fiskárdo; tel: 26740 41203.* If you are looking for somewhere central, these six reasonably priced rooms are above a restaurant right on Fiskárdo's picturesque waterfront – worth the price for the location alone.

Recommended Restaurants

Restaurants in resort areas are typically open only during the high season (mid-June to October). Those in the bigger towns are open all year round, but most of them shut at least one day a week.

Unless otherwise indicated, traditional establishments generally open for lunch from noon until around 3.30pm and for dinner from 7pm to around 11.30pm. More tourist-oriented establishments open early for breakfast or coffee and stay open throughout the day.

If you are planning a special journey to dine during low season, it's always advisable to call to confirm. Reservations are necessary only at top restaurants in high season or on Sunday at lunchtime. If a telephone number is not provided, it is because reservations are not taken. Staff at a typical *tavérna* will usually bring out more tables and chairs rather than turn you away.

The following prices reflect the average cost of a two-course meal (per person) and a half bottle of wine. The most expensive restaurants add a service charge to your bill (usually around 10 percent), but the vast majority of restaurants do not. However, at all restaurants an automatic tax of 18 percent (VAT) is always included in the prices listed on the menu. It is customary to leave an additional five to 10 percent for the waiter, especially if they are an employee and not the owner.

€€€	over 28 euros
€€	17–28 euros
€	below 17 euros

ZÁKYNTHOS

ZÁKYNTHOS TOWN

Akrotiri Taverna €€ *Akrotíri, 4km (2½ miles) north of Zákynthos Town; tel: 26950 45712.* A pleasant summer-only *tavérna* with a large garden. Grilled meats are a speciality, but staff also bring round large trays of tempting *mezédes* from which you pick and choose. Prices are reasonable, and the house wine is more than acceptable.

Arekia €–€€ *Dionysíou Romá (the Repáro coast road); tel: 26950 26346.* Smoky, unpretentious hole-in-the-wall, opened just after the 1953 earthquake and fitting around 70 diners cosily on bench seats, evenings only all year. The food's good but incidental to the main event: *kandádes* and *arékia* singing after 10pm.

Komis €€–€€€ *Bastoúni tou Agíou; tel: 26950 26915.* A lovely *psarotavérna* tucked into a rather unlikely spot behind the port authority building (opposite Agíou Dionysíou). The emphasis is on slightly pricey but fresh and inventive fish and seafood dishes, but there is a good list of *mezédes*, good wine and, better still, tempting desserts.

Malanos € *Agíou Athanasíou 38, Kípi district (south of the river); tel: 26950 45936.* A deservedly popular and inexpensive all-year shrine of *magirevtá*; mince-rich *youvarlákia* and *fasolákia yahní* are typical offerings. There's also unusually good bread as well as the expected barrel wine. The green, low-traffic surroundings are the envy of more central *tavérnes*.

VASILIKÓS AND LAGANÁS BAY

Agnadi Taverna €€ *beyond Argási, 8km (5 miles) from Zákynthos Town; tel: 26950 35183.* An attactive modern wooden building on a steep slope overlooking the sea. It is slightly touristy, but the home cooking is authentic and tasty. The menu covers the generic standards, but also has some interesting specials.

Taverna 'Dennis' €€ *Lithakiá; tel: 26950 51387.* A bit of an institution, and open all year round, Dennis's is a friendly, long-standing eatery serving decent standard *tavérna* food. Things to go for include grilled octopus, various souvláki and the salads; the house wine isn't bad either. However, if you feel so inclined, this is one of the better places for a 'Greek night' *(see page 90)*. There is also free transport back to your villa or hotel.

Theodoritsis €€–€€€ *just past Argási in Vasilikós municipal territory; tel: 26950 48500, mobile: 694 4135560.* Theodoritsis is where the *beau monde* of Zákynthos go for a weekend blowout; the stress on *magirevtá* but grills and *mezédes* are also available. Moderately pricey. Summer terrace overlooking town and tasteful interior. Open all year.

Zakanthi €€ *Kalamáki; tel: 26950 43586.* This is probably the most attractive place to eat in Kalamáki, with dining in a large well-maintained garden. The food, which is quite good, is a mix of pasta, pizza and the usual Greek offerings (grills and salads). Once the sun has gone down and the subdued lighting comes on in the garden, it is lovely here.

THE NORTH

Alitzerini €€ *entrance to Kilioméno; tel: 26950 48552.* Housed in one of the few surviving 17th-century Venetian village houses, this little *inomagerío* offers hearty, meat-based country cooking and (as ever) its own wine; *kandádes* some evenings. Evenings only: Fri–Sun Oct–May, daily June–Sept. Reservations essential. During the day, head for **Korfiatos**, a wooden balcony at the top of the hill with lovely views. Here you can have a drink or simple meal. Behind the benches are huge barrels of local wine, as well as excellent local oil and thyme honey for sale.

Andreas €€ *Paralía Beloúsi, near Drosiá; tel 26950 61604.* A no-nonsense fish *tavérna* with a patently fresh catch at fair prices, said by locals to be the best on the island. During summer there is terrace seating by the sea. To go with the fish there is good bread, delicious boiled *kolokythákia* (courgettes) and passable wine.

Andreas Zontas €€–€€€ *Pórto Limniónas, Ágios Léon.* Location can count for a lot, and this *estiatório* must have one of the best on the island. The food is relatively expensive, standard *tavérna* fare, but it is served on a promontory overlooking an idyllic rocky bay and faces west to the sunset.

Kalas €–€€ *Kabí, in the village before the road climbs up to the headland. No tel.* Kalas is by far the best *tavérna* in Kabí – the others, located on the headland, serve substandard food to coachloads of tourists bussed in to see the sunset. Kalas is set in a pretty garden, shaded by large trees, and serves up all the usual favourites (*fáva*, *loukánika*, *horiátiki* and *patátes*), but all are tasty and freshly cooked. Good bulk wine as well.

Mikrinisi €€ *Kokkínou, 1km (½ mile) beyond Makrýs Gialós. No tel.* Standard, but reasonable, *tavérna* food – *horiátiki*, *kalamarákia*, *souvláki* and the like – but served in a delightful setting. The *tavérna* is perched on the edge of a small headland overlooking a tiny harbour, and you can watch the boats bobbing in the inlet as you eat.

Rouli's €€ *Kypséli Beach, near Drosiá; tel: 26950 61628.* A friendly place overlooking the sea and a narrow beach – and popular with islanders – Rouli's gets very fresh fish (one of its main attractions) but also has a good line in the usual Greek salads and vegetables. The house wine is drinkable, and the freshness of all the ingredients make a trip here well worth the detour off the main road.

Théatro Avoúri Estiatorio €–€€ *just north of Limodaíka near Tragáki. No tel.* This is a gorgeous and informal place for a meal, a stone-built open-air theatre complex set in lovely countryside. The local food is cooked in a traditional oven – producing tempting aromas and excellent bread – and you can also catch one of the storytelling performances. Open every night from around 7pm onwards.

To Fanari tou Keriou €€€ *1.5 km (1 mile) beyond Kerí village, on southwest tip of island; tel: 26950 43384, mobile: 697 2676302.* Worth the trip out, especially on nights when you can watch the full moon rise over the sea-stacks known as the Myzíthres. The food's on the expensive side, but portions are fair size and quality is high – try vegetable-stuffed *pandséta*, redolent of nutmeg, and daily-made *galaktoboúreko*. Reservations essential.

KEFALLONIA

ARGOSTÓLI

There are a few places on or just off Platía Vallianoú that are good for breakfast, a snack or for simply sitting with a drink. **Premiere**, between Hotel Aenos and the Ionian Plaza, advertises itself as a *crêperie-gelaterie* but is not a bad place for breakfast (even if the service is very slow). Better is **Siora Kate**, just up the hill at K. Vergóti 9, a small but popular bakery serving tasty savoury pies and *bougátsa*. Of the cafés surrounding the square, the **Central Café** (tel: 26710 26680), on the corner near the Foká-Kosmetátou Foundation, is one of the most pleasant.

Kyani Akti €€€ *A. Trítsi 1, far end of the quay; tel: 26710 26680.* A superb, if pricey, *psarotavérna* built out over the sea. The speciality is, unsurprisingly, fresh fish and seafood, and they often have unusual things to try (including the utterly delicious *dáktylia* – 'fingers' – which are akin to razor clams). All the fish and seafood is sold by weight (you go and pick it from the buckets at the back), but there is also a range of *mezédes* and salads, and some tasty house wine.

Maïstrato €–€€ *far north end of quay by fishing anchorage; tel: 26710 26563.* Set yourself up at this genuine *ouzerí* with a seafood *pikilía* (medley), some of their abundant hot/cold *mezédes* and *oúzo* by the 200-ml carafe. Very reasonable, pleasant waterside seating beside a pine grove (take mosquito repellent, as these insects can be quite fierce here). Apr–Oct only.

Mr 'Grillo' €€ *A. Trítsi 135. No tel.* A *psistariá*, not far from the port authority building, and very popular with the locals for Sunday lunch. The grilled meats are tasty, as are the accompanying *mezédes*, and it's all reasonably priced, though the service can be a little surly when things get busy.

Patsouras € *A. Trítsi 32 (north quay); tel: 26710 22779.* Popular *magirevtá* specialist just along from the Lixoúri ferry (look for the lurid green sign). Good ribsticking food, with especially tasty *bámies* (okra), a few grills and big portions, and there is velvety red house wine. It's open all year.

To Kafenio tis Kabanas € *Lithóstroto 52B; tel: 26710 24456.* Housed in a reconstructed Venetian tower and with seating in the square opposite, this pleasant café serves light snacks. Run by the local ROTA cooperative, it helps place people with mental-health problems back in jobs and the community. As well as the usual run of coffees there are a few local specialities, such as *soumáda* (an orgeat drink) and *amygdalópita* (almond pie).

To Steki €–€€ *Rizospáston.* A good-value, friendly little place close to Platía Vallianoú. There is seating on the pavement, or in the attractively plain traditional interior. The tasty, well-cooked food is simple, running to dishes such as *fáva*, *patátes*, salads, a few fresh fish dishes and some grilled meats. Open all day.

LIXOÚRI AND THE SOUTH

Akrogiali € *Lixoúri quay (Andréa Laskarátou), towards south end; tel: 26710 92613.* An enduring, budget-priced institution, with largely local clientele. Wholesome and tasty food with a stress on oven-casserole food (including *giouvétsi*, *kreatópita* and great *hórta*), but also fish and grills in the evening, plus excellent bulk wine.

Blue Sea (alias Spyros') €€€ *Káto Katélios; tel: 26710 81353.* The speciality here is pricey, but fresh and superbly grilled, fish from the little anchorage adjacent. Budget about €30 each for a large portion with a share of *mezédes* and their bulk wine. Credit cards are accepted.

Remetzo € *Póros, over the headland by the port; tel: 26740 72691.* A pleasant café-cum-*gelaterie* just by the rocks of the headland and overlooking the harbour. It serves basic snacks (such as omelettes) and huge ice-creams. The very clean toilets are definitely a bonus.

Romantza €€ *Póros, southern end of the town beach; tel: 26740 72294.* This *estiatório* is in a delightful position, built into the headland at the end of the town beach. You eat on a first-storey balcony, which has views over the sea to Itháki. The focus of the menu is on a large range of fresh fish (priced by weight), but there are also good *mezédes* and salads.

Ta Delfina €–€€ *Sámi waterfront. No tel.* A basic but pleasant waterfront place with daily *magirevtá* such as *briám* (similar to ratatouille), *giouvétsi* and good *hórta*. There is also some fresh fish, usually small tasty offerings including sardines, octopus and *marídes*. This is about the best in a line of rather touristy places, all with outdoor seating overlooking the harbour.

Tsivas € *Póros, over the headland by the port. No tel.* A seafood and meat-grill specialist, with seating perched overlooking the fishing port and spectacular coastal scenery. The food is tasty and fairly basic, but it is hygienic and inexpensive. Only open during high season.

THE NORTH

Ionio Psisteria €–€€ *Mánganos, just after the turn-off to Matsoukáta. No tel.* A pleasant, unpretentious roadside restaurant about 10km (6 miles) before Fiskárdo. Very reasonable, the food is honest and tasty, especially the *mousakás*, and the service is friendly. Seating is either inside the traditional little building, or on the roadside veranda. On Saturdays they spit-roast a whole pig.

Nirides €€ *Ásos, the far end of the harbour; tel: 26740 51467.* A little *estiatório*, one in a line overlooking the very attractive harbour. There is the usual range of salads and a few grilled and oven dishes, as well as fresh fish by the kilo. However, it is all well cooked – especially the fried peppers with cheese and *melidzánes imám* – and the location is great. If this place is full (and it does get crowded), try the **Estiatorio Platanos** on Platía Parísion behind the waterfront, set around a large tree; this second restaurant is popular with visiting Greeks and has a huge range of reasonable food.

Paradisenia Akti (Stavros Dendrinos) €€ *far east corner of Agía Evfimía resort, above 'Paradise Beach'; tel: 26740 61392*. Fair-priced, savoury dishes such as *hortópita* and local sausage, though the seafood portions could be bigger; lovely terrace seating under pines and grape arbours, overlooking the sea.

Tassia €€€ *northwest side of quay, Fiskárdo; tel: 26740 41205*. Although overpriced, this place attracts a celebrity clientele, so is worth it if you're looking for a touch of glamour. You can easily spend €40–50 a head if you go for lobster dishes and other seafood, but you can also get out of the door for €25–30 each by sharing *mezédes* in a group. It's not all it's cracked up to be, though – the *briám* is overblown, and the mozzarella, basil and tomato salad is to be avoided at all costs. Tassia Dendrinou, the owner, does a weekly television cooking show in Athens. Open most of the year.

To Foki € *at the head of Fóki Bay. No tel*. This is a very pleasant *tavérna*, friendly and just opposite the beach. It serves simple but tasty food – *fáva*, *souvláki* and *salads* – and lovely *milópita* (apple pie). Much better, and far cheaper, than anything to be found in Fiskárdo just down the road. Take mosquito repellent for the evenings.

To Pevko €€ *Andipáta Erísou, just by the turning for Dafnoúdi beach; tel: 26740 41360*. A serious contender for the best place to eat on the island. The seating is outside under a huge pine tree, which becomes nicely atmospheric at dusk. The women in the kitchen are geniuses, cooking a mouthwatering selection of *mezédes*, oven-cooked dishes and some grilled meat and fish. Particularly good are the tomato, mint and féta *'keftédes'*, the *gígandes* (butter beans) and aubergine with garlic. For dessert don't miss the (hot) *fýllo* covered ice cream with sour cherries. As a bonus, the beer glasses are kept in the freezer.

Vasso's €€–€€€ *southeast end of quay, Fiskárdo; tel: 06740 41276*. *Magirevtá* with a difference: olive tapinade for your bread, dill and other herbs flavour many of the dishes, and there is seafood pasta and creative desserts. Reasonable (for Fiskárdo anyway) at about €25 each if you stay away from lobster.

INDEX

(Z) indicates places on Zákynthos
(K) indicates places on Kefalloniá
(I) indicates places on Itháki